SAM FAIERS
My Baby & Me

My Secrets to
Surviving Life as
a New Mum

BLINK
bringing you closer

Published by Blink Publishing
3.08, The Plaza,
535 Kings Road,
Chelsea Harbour,
London, SW10 0SZ

www.blinkpublishing.co.uk

facebook.com/blinkpublishing
twitter.com/blinkpublishing

Hardback – 978-1-911-274-65-0
Trade paperback – 978–1–911–274–89–6
Paperback – 978-1-911-600-17-6
Ebook – 978-1-911-274-66-7

A CIP catalogue of this book is available from the British Library.

Design and typeset by seagulls.net
Printed and bound by Clays Ltd, St. Ives Plc

1 3 5 7 9 10 8 6 4 2

Blink Publishing is an imprint of the Bonnier Publishing Group
www.bonnierpublishing.co.uk

SAM FAIERS

is a reality TV star, businesswoman, bestselling author, model and mum. She starred in the hit show *The Only Way is Essex* and was a finalist on *Celebrity Big Brother*. She owns Minnies Boutique along with online fashion retailer, All Bits London, and also has her own bestselling range of beauty products. As well as appearing in her own series on ITVBe, *The Mummy Diaries*, Sam is a blossoming photographer and hosts her own YouTube channel.

PRAISE FOR
My Baby & Me

'As funny as they are emotional, Sam's experiences in this intimate read will offer comfort and advice to others in the same situation… Sam really shows off the reality of being a mum' *MummyPages*

'[*My Baby & Me*] covers from bump to baby with amazing insights into getting back into shape, to breastfeeding struggles, to holidays, weaning and so much more … a great read for all parents' *Twinderelmo* blog

For my two Pauls – you're my everything
and I love you both so much

Contents

Foreword

Dear Mums, Mums-to-be and anyone else who is reading this,

Firstly, I want to say the Mum Club is the best membership I've ever had – it beats a posh members-only club any day! It's a club where you stop being the only thing you think about, a club where you celebrate how brilliant your body is and a club where you realise what unconditional love really means.

I always knew I wanted children, but I didn't realise I would adore being a mum as much as I do – there genuinely isn't anything like it in the world and nothing can prepare you for how much your life will change.

When I got pregnant, and maybe because I am fairly young, I had a lot of people telling me their horror stories – how my life was over, that I would lose my figure, how my relationship would suffer as me and Paul hadn't been together that long. The list went on and on, and although most did agree that the love you have for your child is like no other and it outweighs everything, it didn't stop people trying to tell me what was what. It also didn't stop them from putting their hands on my bump and touching my stomach. But to be honest I didn't mind that too much. In fact, every time the baby kicked I made whoever I was with put their hand on my tummy to feel it!

Actually, I have learned that the best thing people can do for you throughout the whole process is to give you space to find your own feet and work out how *you* want to do things. However unprepared you think you are, as soon as you give birth, a mother's instinct kicks in and it takes over.

Obviously I had seen my sister Billie have Nelly and welcoming her into the family was amazing for us all. During Nelly's first year I was round at Billie's every day and saw up close how demanding it could be. I had gone through Billie's pregnancy with her and been there at the birth, which was so magical, and then been fully involved during those precious first weeks and months. Now it is so lovely because Nelly and Paul see each other nearly every day – they are more like brother and sister than cousins. She is so good with him and his little face lights up when he sees her. It is the cutest thing, and a good way of preparing Nelly for being an actual big sister and sharing the limelight!

I knew motherhood was mind-blowing, but until it happens to you, there is no way of knowing how you will feel because everyone is different. That's the main thing I want to reassure you about: we all do things our own way, and only we can know our bodies and our babies. My biggest piece of advice is to take your time to get to know your baby and just go with your gut.

Obviously it is a daunting time – with your first baby you are stepping into the unknown and everything is new – and it is scary being responsible for such a tiny baby who relies on you for everything. That's why I wanted to do this book. I had lots of great advice but having a baby has brought out my stubborn side: it made me determined to do it my way! Of course I looked a lot of stuff up and took advice from my mum, Gaynor (Paul's mum) and Billie, but in the end, you've got to do what's right for you and I really wish there had been a book to tell me that. Being a first-time mum doesn't mean you can't do what feels right, even if you don't have any previous experience.

There are so many blogs and books out there that can make everything look as picture perfect as an *OK!* shoot, but that isn't real life with a newborn baby. What you didn't see is all the unsorted washing hidden in the spare room, or that, in the pictures showing me just from the waist up, I was wearing Paul's socks and my slippers for comfort. No one has any idea how much time and effort goes into making those natural 'at home' magazine shoots look relaxed. Believe me, at the time of my 'introducing the baby to the world' shoot there was nothing glamorous about how I was feeling – I was wearing layers of make-up to hide the dark circles and had some-thing green on my bra! Wearing high heels and make-up was the last thing on my agenda – it was a miracle I washed my hair and got out of my tracksuit!

The main thing I want to reassure you about is that this book isn't full of dos and don'ts, it won't tell you that I was back in my size 8 jeans within a week of having baby Paul and that he has just 'slotted right in' so I didn't even notice I'd had a baby. It won't tell you he was sleeping from 7pm to 7am in his perfectly kitted out nursery from the age of six weeks, or that me and Paul went on a romantic weekend away when he was three months old to celebrate 'getting back to normal'. Having a baby changes everything overnight, it is the toughest, most tiring thing, but it changes things for the better. My only advice is to find your own way through and discover what works for *you*. While I was pregnant, I had so many questions but all the books and blogs I read were either too fluffy, too technical or too full of rules that made me feel inferior and on the back foot from the start. When you are about to tackle something new you want to be reassured that the person you are taking advice from has been in your shoes. Trust me, I have, and the shoes don't miraculously fit as soon as you bring the baby home – I'm still getting used to wearing mine!

The arrival of a baby changes both parents and the relationship you have. All I can say about us is that baby Paul brought us closer than ever. We just love him so much and we look at each other differently. We are parents now and we are so excited to have more babies and grow our family. I knew from the moment I had baby Paul that I could never go back to being the woman I'd been before. Paul often says that life changed forever at the hospital from the very minute baby Paul arrived, that you don't think you can love each other any more and then suddenly there is this baby who needs you both for everything. He says that he slipped right into wanting to protect us both and I felt the same – it became all about our family, protecting and loving the baby and the life we were going to build together. Becoming a mum has made me feel both really vulnerable and very empowered – knowing that you would do anything to protect your baby makes you feel like you can take on the world. You grow up instantly.

This book is about my journey and how I experienced pregnancy and baby Paul's first year. Obviously, as his dad, Paul is a huge part of that, but the book is mainly from my point of view. You've seen some of it on TV in *The Baby Diaries* and most recently *The Mummy Diaries*, and a little glimpse on my social media, but here are the highs, lows and everything in between. This is what worked for me in my words, from an honest mum just trying to tell it how it is. I'm not saying it's the right way, it's just my way. You might not even have a baby, but are just reading this to find out how was is for me. Whatever stage you are at in your lives, thank you for buying my book.

Becoming a mum is the biggest, most overwhelming thing you can do in your life, but also the best. Welcome to my family.

Love, Sam x

Prologue

I knew deep down, I suppose. You just know when something is different with your body.

I have really regular periods. I've always been like clockwork from the minute they started, so being late was the biggest give-away for me. I gave it two days before I told Paul what I suspected. We both had these really nervous grins on our faces – a complete mixture of fear and excitement but nerves too, and the weirdness of not knowing for sure. He kept asking me what I thought and if I had any other symptoms; and I remembered that morning in the shower being under the hot water and my nipples starting to tingle, which felt odd and certainly wasn't anything I had ever experienced before. I believe women have a sixth sense about these things and what is going on with their bodies.

The morning I decided to do the pregnancy test I'd been at home in my tracksuit doing paperwork for the shop. As soon as I told Paul how I felt and that I thought I might be pregnant we just kept looking at each other and laughing, so I decided to go down to the local chemist and get a test to find out for sure. I had my scruffs on and my hair scraped back, and it was a bit of a gamble – going into the shop and buying something so obvious – but I had to know for sure. Thank God nobody saw me and took a picture or Snapchatted it! Looking back, it would have made more sense to send Paul to the chemist, as he'd have been relatively unrecognisable to photographers at that time. (As will be pointed out a lot in this book, we had only just started dating when I got pregnant. It was so early on in our relationship that the press hadn't really even worked out who he was!)

I ran home and went straight upstairs to the bathroom, took the test out of all the many layers of plastic packaging (why so many layers when most people taking the test will be impatient to find out either way?!) and weed on it right away. Within about 15 seconds, it came up positive. It is really hard to explain how I felt; because we weren't technically 'trying', there wasn't that desperation to see the blue lines, but because we weren't actively preventing it either, I suppose a part of me hoped it was positive and was excited at the thought. I just got this nervous laugh and Paul kept saying: 'Are you sure, Sam? Are you REALLY sure?'

It was a crazy mixture of happiness and joy, as well as being scared at this new path we were on. We had been dating for four months – that's only 16 weeks!! And here we were, having a baby. The reality was that we didn't really have a clue about what was coming our way and how our lives would change forever.

Meeting
Mr Right

I suppose that in many ways, until I met Paul, life had been a bit of an Essex cliché. It had been all spray tans, nail gels, being followed by cameras and Sugar Hut club antics. Living your life out on a reality TV show can be tough and I think everyone knows how my story went before I settled down with Paul.

Part of my decision to leave *The Only Way is Essex* was to find a different career path, but also get some control over my private life and meet someone I could genuinely build a future with. I knew I wasn't going to find that person on the show, and that it was time to grow up and move on. When you live in Essex it is easy to get drawn into the drama, and it was fun but the Sam you saw on screen wasn't the real me. It was like playing a part I'd outgrown and I was ready to leave it behind.

It still makes me laugh that, despite wanting to move away from the small, cliquey world I inhabited, meeting Paul was a classic Essex fairy tale. It is so ironic that we first set eyes on each other in the restaurant Sheesh (which is always on social media and full of the *TOWIE* cast), having been introduced by Ferne McCann from *TOWIE*. Talk about keeping it local!

Everything about Paul and me has been a fast-forward whirl-wind right from the very start. I know it sounds cheesy, but from the minute I clapped eyes on him, I just knew. I was standing with Ferne and she was saying, 'There's that guy I was telling you about, the one I bet you'd fancy.'

She had seen him out and about a few times and had decided that we were bound to like each other. Ferne and me have known each other for years and she knows better than anyone that my type is tall, dark and handsome. Paul was standing at the bar with his brother and his mate, chatting and laughing; he had lovely eyes and a great smile. At first, it was so busy and crowded in the restaurant that I couldn't work out exactly which of the three blokes Ferne was pointing at, but as soon as she told me Paul was the one in the middle, I was drawn to him right away. I fancied him the moment I saw him. I loved the way he dressed. He had a nice suede jacket on, lovely shoes and jeans that fitted him well. He looked so manly, with loads of curly hair and totally my type. I think when you are that attracted to someone, you know immediately, and I knew within the first week we were going to be together.

I know a lot of people were shocked at how quickly things moved between us, but we fell in love straight away and talked about babies from day one. I've never made any secret about the fact I wanted to be a mummy and it was something that Paul wanted too – luckily, or it could have been a bit awkward given where we are now!

I always think the phrase 'trying for a baby' is a weird one and I don't think we were doing that, but we weren't going to great efforts to make sure it didn't happen either, if you know what I mean. I know lots of people don't understand the idea of 'seeing what happens' when it comes to getting pregnant or trying for a baby – if you don't take steps to stop pregnancy, chances are you will get pregnant! I think in our case, it was so early on in our relationship that perhaps we didn't want to admit that we were ready for such a huge step; perhaps we were just well and truly in the honeymoon phase and not paying close enough attention. Lots of people couldn't understand the rush and I know that, technically, we had all the time in the world, but we both knew we wanted to make a family together. Paul is the best daddy to our son and the biggest support to me, which means even more given that in previous relationships I have always had to lead the way and be the one in charge of everything. I love that it is different with Paul – I feel looked after and it just felt right from the very first date.

I'm not going to lie: I know that getting pregnant within four months of meeting someone isn't the norm, and from the minute I took the test and saw it was positive I felt really spaced out. That moment when you realise it is really happening to you feels like a real blur. It is so much to take in and a hundred thoughts whizz through your brain, but the one thing we immediately agreed on was to keep it to ourselves for a few weeks. I think we just needed to process what was happening and the fact it was real!

Once we had started to get our heads around it, we told my sister and my mum. Telling Billie was hilarious – we were standing in her kitchen, Nelly was crying, Billie was getting dinner ready and

I was struggling to get my words out. Finding the right moment to tell people is hard enough but I also have a real issue with the word 'pregnant'! Don't ask me why, but I find it such a weird word to say and also, when I'm nervous, I get the giggles. All in all, it was hard to say it out loud – Billie was putting a casserole in the oven and so I just blurted it out. She nearly dropped the dish in shock. In fact, that was the reaction I got from most people! Billie cried and so did my mum when I told her. She just stood there, mouth open, saying: 'Is it true, is it true?'

She just couldn't believe it and she really wasn't expecting to be a nanny again so soon. She was still getting to know Paul and it took a while for her to get used to the news. I told my dad a few weeks after Mum and Billie and he was really emotional, but I was still really surprised when he cried. I know he and Paul are very different but they get on and I know Dad is happy I am settled with someone who looks after me. Now we have had baby Paul, the only question my dad has is, 'When's the wedding?'

I know that's how Paul's mum Gaynor feels as well. Despite the fact we have been close from the moment we met, she is a born-again Christian and has strong views, which I totally respect. I know in an ideal world she would have liked us to be husband and wife before the baby came along, but that said, I couldn't have asked for a better support from her. She's like a second mother to me and we couldn't be closer. Baby Paul is her first grandchild and she dotes on him. Between her, my mum and Billie, sometimes me and Paul don't get a look in!

At first, we didn't really tell anyone apart from immediate family – I don't know why we did it that way looking back, but it was really nice to have something for ourselves. It was a shock and I think that time just allowed us to process and get used to the news before all the questions started and before we also had to deal with the press. In those early days it can be a bit overwhelming, but also coping with the opinions of strangers and journalists can be tough, and seeing the news online and in magazines can be a bit hard.

Having said that, when I found out I was pregnant there was never one second where I thought we can't do this. It didn't cross my mind. Paul is really laid-back – we don't argue or scream and shout, that's just not what we are like. Our personalities are similar in many ways and we complement each other: we are what each other was looking for in a partner. Paul is very old school and old-fashioned, he's all about protecting his family, which is so refreshing as that quality is hard to find in a lot of blokes today. I will be honest and say that it is nice to have that pressure taken off me by someone who wants to look out for me for once. People might criticise me for saying that but it is truly how I feel: I am proud to say that as a couple we are quite old-fashioned. In my family when I was young, rightly or wrongly, the women in my life did the cooking and cleaning and the men went out to work – that's what I had growing up. All I know is that Paul wants the best for me and baby Paul, and he will do all he can to provide for us.

We have had our fair share of stick, and that has been hard – I think I got more offended than Paul, who would tell me it was fine and he could handle it. I get that our way isn't for everyone, but I am a great believer in live and let live.

Personally, I think it is really hard for my generation to find in a man what our dads provided for us when we were young – a man to hold the door, support you and have your back no matter what, but I have found that in Paul. Gaynor brought up Paul and his brother Tony on her own, and they are a credit to her. She was very strict with them, and they are very loyal and loving. I felt accepted by her right from the word go, and she has welcomed me into her family like I am one of her own. Since I have had baby Paul she has taught me so much, as has my mum and Billie. I feel really lucky that I have such a strong unit around me. I suppose that's my first piece of advice: keep the people you trust close to you in those early weeks – you will need them.

But before I get ahead of myself, at the time it was like a bomb had gone off. If someone had asked me how I felt, I would have said scared, worried, excited and overwhelmed all at the same time – basically, all the gear and no idea.

Going Public

I know that I am not Kim Kardashian in terms of media interest, but the way the press found out about my pregnancy wasn't great and I suppose our first baby milestone was made hard by the fact I was in the public eye.

After we had told our immediate family, we decided to keep it quiet. I had no cravings, no sickness, no bump really! I felt that over the years I had shared so much about myself, and so we decided that this was our news and we would tell it when we wanted. I guess that's another piece of advice: it's your body and your news, so make sure you tell people when you want to. Just because the 12 weeks are up it doesn't mean you need to tell the world if you aren't ready – I waited five months to tell any of my friends, and in the end the press leaked it anyway.

Why did I keep it quiet for so long? I suppose there was a part of me that worried people would judge the short amount of time me and Paul had been together. Let's face it: everyone has an opinion, whether or not they know you, especially where I live and most definitely if you are in the public eye. Essex is full of gossip and other people's opinions – we didn't want anything to burst our happy bubble.

Obviously we had to spend some time talking things through. The pregnancy was a huge deal, and we needed to process what it meant for us and how we felt about it before we had quick answers for the media – I just didn't feel in the right headspace for the Spanish Inquisition. The plan was to go on one last holiday for a bit of private time while it was still our little secret, and then do a nice Instagram post with a picture of us and our own words describing how excited we were when we got back at the end of August. I still didn't really look pregnant, more like I'd eaten too much food, so it wasn't hard to keep people off the scent. We were away in Majorca having some time to ourselves when all hell broke loose. Somehow, the story was leaked.

The *Mirror* had got hold of the news that I was pregnant and they knew I was well over three months. How they got that information I will never know. It took something away from the moment – that was our milestone to cherish and reveal when we were ready. Things like that bring home the downside of being in the public eye. I guess your life does become headline fodder for people to gossip about and people can earn a quick buck from selling those private times to papers desperate for stories. It goes with the territory, but it was especially hard this time as it affected both of our families – and Paul's family was new to the fame game.

I felt so bad for Paul. He had to make some panicked calls to his family and friends to tell them we were having a baby before they read about it while they ate their breakfast the next day. It wasn't how he imagined telling the people close to him that he was going to be a daddy and I felt so guilty that I had brought him into my world, but we were determined not to let it spoil our moment. So the story ran, we made our statement and then took back some control by talking to *OK!* and doing a 'bump reveal'. Doing a shoot like that is a great way to get across your own, true version of events – you can't be misquoted and it is also really nice to get some lovely pictures to mark the big milestones. I know that some people criticise celebrities for doing these shoots for things like weddings etc., but sometimes it really is the only way to make sure you have your say on what's happening in your life.

It was an odd feeling, getting all glammed up in heels, make-up and crop tops to show off the bump – I was wearing things I would never normally have been seen dead in walking down the street! My bump was so small at that time I kept trying to stick it out more for the photos – on set I was eating loads and drinking cup after cup of peppermint tea. I had a massive sausage sandwich just so I would bloat out!

Some of this shoot was filmed for *The Baby Diaries* and it was clear what a different world this was for Paul – it was there everyone could see how protective he was of me. Paul wasn't very comfortable with my baby bump being exposed. He used to say that it was some-thing very sacred to him and not for others to see. Coming from his world to mine was, and is still, hard, as it is very, very different and I have had years of practice, while he was thrown in at the deep end. Just as he was getting used to going out with me and being papped, then suddenly everyone was writing about us having a baby and trying to get shots of my bump. He went from hard hats and building sites to sitting in make-up chairs and seeing himself on the cover of *OK!*. Getting used to that, as well as the prospect of soon becoming a daddy, was tough on him, but he is a strong man. We may have only been together a short amount of time, but we were strong and ready for the adventure.

Things that surprised me about being pregnant:

- It isn't the same for everyone but some of the old wives' tales were true for me – I had no sickness, no cravings and no mood swings, but I did carry my bump weight all at the front, which they reckon means it is a boy.

- The nesting thing is SO true – but I didn't wait until the end for it to kick in, I had it all the way through. I cleared out bags of clothes and shoes for the whole nine months! I became a total homebody and was obsessed with getting the house repainted and fresh carpets laid for when the baby was born.

- My hair and skin was the best it has ever been – I was so lucky I didn't get the pregnancy acne that Billie got with Nelly.

- Water retention is REAL! I was fine right until the end and then I just blew up like a whale, I was literally double the size. Me and Paul used to look at my feet and compare them to pigs' trotters! I couldn't have worn any of my heels even if I'd wanted to (and I didn't).

- Your body really will tell you what it needs – make sure you listen to it and eat what you fancy, when you fancy it.

Pregnancy – the Reality

I won't lie: I had a lovely pregnancy. I know people probably want to hear horror stories, but I don't have any – it was one of the happiest times of my life.

The best way I can describe it is that for the first three months it is like your body is on lockdown as it prepares for everything that's about to happen, all the changes and strains that are coming your way. I could feel my body changing massively almost immediately. I was so tired and felt a bit rough during the first trimester, but once I got through that bit the energy kicked in and, until the very end when everything got swollen, I was on the go. I wasn't sick and didn't have any cravings apart from the final few weeks when I became addicted to spearmint after stealing a mint from someone! That was the only thing I became a bit obsessive about. I certainly didn't go down the pickles route and my diet was totally normal all the way through.

I know that I was really lucky – poor Kate Middleton gets so sick and some people have a miserable time. I didn't have any of the early symptoms that some women get, including mood swings, extreme tiredness, a metallic taste, agonisingly sore boobs or feeling faint. It felt like business as usual, which was just as well, given we hadn't told people outside of our imemdiate families.

The biggest thing for me was that my mind was so clear. I had made some changes to my management team and day-to-day set-up, I felt like my brain was so organised and I was very creative – I worked out what I wanted to do and where I wanted to be with work stuff, and that was an amazing feeling. I had bags of energy and did loads of forward planning with my boutique Minnies and other stuff I had on the go. I was buzzing and couldn't believe how much energy and clarity I had. I felt driven and ready to embrace the next stage of what was to come.

The reason for this was probably much more mundane than being pregnant. For a start, I was properly sober for the first time in a long time. I had been a party girl who enjoyed going out and about with my friends and having a few drinks – what young girl doesn't? There is a stage in every girl's life where all you do is focus on where you are going, what you are wearing, what club you are going to meet at and who you are going to meet, and that takes up a lot of headspace. When you're pregnant, suddenly all that is gone and you have the space to think about serious things like nurturing a baby and making a future with the man you love. I found it so liberating and exciting – I felt properly grown up.

The biggest immediate and obvious change from taking a break from my party lifestyle was the fact that I didn't wake up with hangovers! After years of never having a break from booze, suddenly I was on an immediate self-imposed detox that lasted the whole pregnancy and six months beyond. My body must have been in shock! I didn't touch booze from the moment the test came up positive, it was one thing I was adamant about. I didn't want to try and drink 'safely' when I was growing my baby – I wanted everything to be pure and to know that everything I was putting into my body was good. I believe you start being a good mum during pregnancy – even though your baby is not on the outside with you, it is your job to nurture your little one as best you can so they are fit and strong for the outside world. From the minute I took the test I felt like a mummy, and from that moment the baby came first.

It was easy giving up drinking as the thought of any alcohol turned my stomach, and it was the last thing I wanted. Being pregnant made me marvel at what my body could do – turning itself off things that aren't good for the growing baby is genius. There might have been an occasion where I was out and people were toasting or saying 'Go on, just have a sip' but my reaction was 'God, no'. I had my first drink when he was seven months and that was a glass of Prosecco, so not exactly a shot fest! At the point I started having a few sips, baby Paul was having meals and going longer between feeds in the day and not needing me so much, so I wasn't as strict with myself. It definitely felt good to relax things a bit and have the odd glass of bubbles with dinner, particularly after baby Paul went to bed.

During the pregnancy, I think my head shifted immediately – like I put myself straight into a 'nesting zone'. I didn't worry about what others were doing and what people were talking about, I was in my own world. I changed the furniture, the lights, got the walls painted fresh and got new carpets. It was important to me for our baby to have a clean slate to come home to. Ideally we would have moved before baby Paul was born – that was the plan, but we couldn't find anywhere we liked (we still can't). But I used the pregnancy as an excuse to have a massive clear-out – not least as Paul had nowhere to put his clothes! I opened a Depop shop and put up loads of clothes, shoes and handbags for sale – it all went and I was brutal. In the end, I had 15,000 items on my page and I gave some of the profits to Haven House; I wanted it to go to a good cause as well as make some much-needed space in my wardrobes. It was nice to say goodbye to the past and get ready for the new.

The spare room (AKA the dumping ground for the clothes that didn't make it to be put away in the wardrobe!) became the nursery but I decided to be a bit restrained. Nelly's room in Billie's house is fit for a princess – there is everything they need in there, and it is so pretty with all her little bits, but we didn't know what we were having so I didn't want to go overboard until we knew what colours to pick. I decided to keep it plain and I was very proud of myself for showing such restraint. We also knew that we wanted to move at some point soon, so it didn't seem worth going to town on making it 'perfect'. In fact, that's another piece of advice I would give: don't worry too much about a catalogue-perfect nursery, in reality you won't use it at all in those first few months. I had everything – the smart white cot, the changing table and matching toy box – but after the first few weeks I was dressing baby Paul on one of the changing mats I kept upstairs and in the living room or on a towel on the bed. After the second month all we used the nursery for was keeping his clothes in his wardrobe and storing his nappies. Our bedroom was where he lived and the nursery was barely touched. If I was doing it again, I wouldn't even convert the spare room at all until baby Paul was a few months old – it would have been better use to us with a bed in it for guests staying over to cook and help!

But back to the pregnancy. It was a bit like I became a new person, like everything I used to think about suddenly didn't matter. All I was focusing on was growing my baby and feeling great, and that involved nourishing my body – it also marked the start of an addiction to avocado! I started eating one a day, which is something I have kept up ever since, and baby Paul loves them too now he's started on solids.

Before I met Paul I had always lived in my house by myself and, as a bit of a party girl, I would often go out rather than cook at home. When I got together with Paul, suddenly I had someone to cook for and Paul loves his food so much. Now I'm with him I eat more than I ever did before, especially since I've been breastfeeding.

Paul introduced me to organic living. Don't get me wrong, we still love a curry and a Chinese, but the rest of the time we eat good, fresh, organic food. We shop at our local farm shop, which sells home-grown and fresh produce – I know I'm lucky to have access to that and I love it all the more now that I'm weaning baby Paul. When I was pregnant, I knew that everything I was putting into my body was somehow going straight to the baby and I felt so strongly that it was my job to give our baby the best start in life.

I have learned so much about food – the hows and whys of what we should eat and what our bodies need. Obviously this is something I first started to explore when I got diagnosed with Crohn's disease – inflammation of the digestive system – and then did more research about when I discovered I was pregnant. I have had so much engagement and support from fans over my diagnosis – lots of people comment on my posts on Instagram asking what I take, what I eat, how I keep flare-ups at bay and a lot of people who have Crohn's wanted to know if I had flare-ups when I was pregnant (I was lucky, I didn't and I haven't really had a major one since having baby Paul either). The truth is that Paul has been a massive help in getting me to understand more about what to eat and how to deal with my condition. After *The Baby Diaries* I got a lot of stick online about me saying that Paul had 'cured' me of Crohn's. What I meant was that all the time he spent researching the disease helped me so much and gave me the confidence to experiment with food and vitamins and see how that helped my health overall.

Paul gave me the confidence to come off the drugs I was put on immediately after I was diagnosed. I was told I had to take azathioprine for life and that it would help control the symptoms – but Paul went out of his way to find natural remedies that would also help me and my body. Rather than just take pills forever, I decided that I wanted to look into other ways of managing things after I was discharged from my private doctor and told I didn't need to come back. I had already come off everything before I got pregnant and then obviously I worked mega hard to maintain this natural way of keeping things at bay once I knew I was pregnant.

I will talk more later on in the book about my diet and how I believe it helps to keep my Crohn's at bay. I will also talk you through the natural remedies that I take every day and why I believe they have helped me so much. Just to be clear, I am not suggesting that people should stop their medication and manage Crohn's with diet and vitamins like me – I'm not a doctor and I'm not qualified to do that. I'm simply sharing what has worked for me and my illness. You can also read up more on Crohn's and pregnancy at the end of the book.

Men and pregnancy

I'm not sure if all men are like this when us girls are pregnant, but the enormity of it all didn't really hit home for Paul until I had a proper bump and, because I didn't really show that much, I think it was hard for him to get that I was pregnant until I was six to seven months gone. When you're first pregnant, you can't wait to show properly – but for the first few months you just look a bit podgy! Once you start to 'pop' out you imagine this neat, hard bump that sticks out perfectly and immediately tells everyone you are expecting, but for a really long time my tummy just wobbled like jelly!

Paul went into full dad mode when I started to show properly – he began talking to the baby and noticing when I was tired. It's obviously much easier for us women to get into the baby zone as we are the ones doing all the hard work, but once I started slowing down, Paul was there for me. We both also loved the scans – it never got any less emotional hearing that heartbeat like loads of horses' hooves – it's the most magical thing and we would have listened to it every day if we could have.

When I finally got one, I loved having a bump, really loved it, and I definitely missed it when I had baby Paul. I used to watch other pregnant women walking down the street and be jealous. It was like our little bond: only I could feel this baby, I was growing him, he kicked only me. It was so weird at first but soon I really looked forward to those reassuring kicks and punches. I got very good at being able to lie on my left side and prod my tummy until I woke him up to play – obviously now he is here and I'm so sleep-deprived, that that's the last thing on my mind!

Paul loved me being pregnant; he used to say that there is something really attractive about pregnant women and that they glowed. I did get the glow halfway through and it made me feel good about my changing body. I think men can underestimate how far a compliment goes in reassuring a pregnant woman when we feel fat and frumpy, especially during that in-between time when nothing fits but there is no actual obvious bump. He was so complimentary to me as my body changed and that gave me a lot of confidence. He has also been brilliant since baby Paul has been here and I have been concentrating on feeding him. I was at my fittest when I met Paul – I trained hard every day and ate well, I had abs and my bum had shape – but all that went out of the window once I fell pregnant. I think it is a mark of how close we are that I didn't worry about it, I simply decided to enjoy my pregnancy and go with the flow.

Working and pregnancy

I know that Paul was worried about me during my pregnancy – I was non-stop, never rested and worried about everything I had to do. He wanted me to slow down and take some time for myself, but that's just not what I am like. He could tell by taking one look at me if I was overdoing it and was too tired. Looking back, I suppose I did try and cram a lot in. I would go from a bump-reveal shoot at a studio with Paul and then straight to Billie's for a shoot with her and Nelly. Then there were photo shoots for the Minnies stock, my other products and endless other things that I do on a daily basis, plus social media posting and going into the shop to serve and have pictures taken with customers.

Other mums might roll their eyes about how manic I was, but I love my job and I take it really seriously. I know that Mum and Billie thought I did too much towards the end – they were happy when I had done my last shift in the shop, as it can get so hectic with people wanting autographs and photos. Minnies is such a tiny space and there was often a scrum – towards the end of my pregnancy I was taking up quite a lot of room! You also don't realise when it's your first baby how valuable time is in those last few weeks before you give birth. You don't understand that the next time you are pregnant you won't be able to lie on the sofa, watching soaps and Netflix, having an afternoon nap and eating. Instead, when I do it again, baby Paul will be toddling around keeping me occupied and on the move. Those last days before baby number one arrives are special – use them to rest up. I know that Billie found pregnancy number two a whole different ball game as she was running around after Nelly all day – you end up going to bed at 7pm!

I did feel like there was pressure to carry on rushing about right up to the end. I'm not sure if that's because my friendship group is quite young and our lives were hectic, or just due to my own expectations. I think having such a good pregnancy meant that I found it hard to moan about much (Paul might disagree!), but I did find it hard to cope with the fact I physically slowed down. I needed to roll myself off the sofa in my final weeks and that wasn't the most attractive sight. I didn't worry too much about losing control over my body – I focused on the end result and saw the weight gain as all being part of the process. I had this idea I would return to exercising straight after the birth and would get back into the best shape of my life – little did I know…

What to Wear...

Fashion-wise I definitely recommend a winter pregnancy! I loved my pregnancy wardrobe: the layering, chunky knits and scarves, the leggings and boots. If you are having an autumn or winter baby, it is much easier to feel comfortable about your body changes under a nice chunky knit cardigan.

There was something really cosy about being indoors, nesting in my sloppy jumpers. In fact, for most of my pregnancy I lived in leggings and a big jumper as they were so comfy and practical for all the examinations as there is minimal clothing to take off. That's the other thing people don't really tell you: you spend a lot of time getting undressed and taking off your underwear!

My body didn't change in a massive way and I didn't put loads of weight on my arms and legs, but the same couldn't be said about my boobs. They were huge and, especially on holiday, I was finding it really hard to dress my chest. I took six different bikinis on our babymoon but didn't try them on before I went and so only realised when I got there that nothing fitted me up top any more. I had to wear and wash out the same bikini top every day as it was the only one that stretched across my giant chest! I found the best place to go for bras to fit my changing boobs was M&S – they do an amazing range of multipack maternity and nursing bras. They are plain cotton and nice and soft, as well as being slightly padded for the support but have no underwiring as I don't like wearing those.

In total I put on two stone. I was having good food on a daily basis and I was eating much more than usual – that hasn't really stopped since baby Paul was born. Your metabolism can change when you are pregnant, but I didn't pile it on and, as annoying as it sounds, it came off fairly quickly afterwards.

I was lucky with my wardrobe, because I didn't get massive I didn't have to change my style and wear much proper maternity gear – imagine strutting down Brentwood High Street in a maternity smock! I enjoyed dressing my bump and as I didn't get huge. I wore stuff that clung a bit, but not too much. Apart from a few essentials like maternity jeans, I just bought normal, non-maternity clothes in a bigger size and that worked perfectly. In fact, I actually decided to use the whole experience to focus on a new business angle by introducing a maternity line at Minnies. By doing that it meant that I could carry on wearing the clothes we sold and posting on social media, which always makes such a huge difference to the business. It made it easier for me to stay totally involved with the shop and also to expand things in a way that reflected the direction my life was going in.

Must-haves for your maternity wardrobe:

- A pair of leggings for every day of the week – they were indispensable! I lived in them by day and smartened them up with a nice top or jacket by night.

- Skinny jeans with the pregnancy band for extra support and comfort were essential. I bought mine from Asos and Mothercare and they were a lifesaver. In fact, I was so obsessed with them that I bought pairs in black, blue and grey. I wore them loads afterwards too, they were perfect for when I was still bloated post-birth and just wanted to feel comfy.

- Nice basic T-shirts made of Lycra that stretched over the bump and made a good shape – perfect when worn with jeans and a smart blazer.

- A chunky knit jumper – a great bump shaper and brilliant for when those hormones make you feel chilly and hot all at the same time!

- Layers – a good loose shirt, thin jumpers and thick scarves will all do the trick to dress a bump.

- Having a nice sexy dress to go out in was really important. Although by day I liked my relaxed look, by night I still loved to feel glam and actually my evening clothes tended to be a bit more fitted and bump-hugging. I wasn't one of those women desperate to hide all signs of pregnancy – I was pregnant and proud!

- Flat shoes – out with the heels and in with the trainers and the flat espadrilles. I don't think I've walked in heels since I got pregnant!

- Nike Flyknit trainers were a MUST-have. I wore them every single day, especially once my feet got so swollen that nothing else would fit. I suppose if it had been summer I would have worn flip-flops, especially when the water retention hit with a vengeance!

My Body

I was lucky in terms of not having cravings or putting on too much weight but that wasn't a conscious decision – I didn't watch what I ate, I just ate really well.

I decided early on that I wanted to be sure that what I was eating was nourishing the baby and making me healthy and strong in order to help me have the labour I wanted. I got really into my breakfasts and started sharing them on Instagram too. I was majorly obsessed with porridge and different toppings, and also loved eggs with lots of different additions like avocado and spices. They filled me up until lunchtime and gave me loads of energy. After that I made sure I had a proper lunch, an afternoon snack, and then cooked for me and Paul in the evening. I also got into my juices and smoothies, a great way to pack in as much goodness as I could – the blender also comes massively in handy now I'm weaning baby Paul. I think that, once I had baby Paul, breastfeeding also meant that I stepped up a gear on the nutrition front as I wanted to get back in shape healthily and at my own pace while also knowing I was giving baby Paul all the nutrients he needed. More of that later.

Before I got pregnant, I felt I was in the best shape of my life. I had been eating well but also exercising loads too – sometimes training five times a week. I had such good intentions to exercise gently while I was pregnant, not least as I thought I would miss it too much as it had become such a part of my everyday life. I couldn't imagine not doing something, however low impact, but the reality was that I did nothing at all, not a bit of anything!

That's the other thing I would stress at this point: do what your body tells you. I did what I had the energy to do and, though I don't recommend going against the guidelines out there, I just did what was best for me. A lot of the stuff that I read told me that I should be exercising gently, trying to fit in 20 minutes a few times a week and getting fit for labour. In the first trimester I was simply too tired to face the thought of working out. Even swimming didn't appeal much and I certainly didn't want to get sweaty. I didn't really bother with my pelvic floor exercises either, though later on in the pregnancy I got a bit more energy and loved going for wintery walks, which helps strengthen your pelvic floor. Then once baby Paul arrived, getting my body back came further down the list than getting to grips with feeding and sleeping. Don't get me wrong, I know I was lucky with my physical health and much of that had to do with my age – we all have different bodies with different needs, I'm just talking from my own experience. Everyone is in different physical shape and will need to follow different paths to get back to feeling healthy and comfortable.

I think this is around the time that I naturally eased off with any kind of unnecessary and time-consuming beauty regime, though actually I had paired my look right back really since before meeting Paul. I had never really been full-on 'big Essex glamour' even when I was on the show – there were always others with blonder and bigger hair, deeper tans or bigger boobs. I wouldn't say I was mega OTT but meeting Paul and feeling very settled gave me the confidence to mess around with my look a bit – my hair went a few shades darker, I lightened up the make-up and experimented with different styles. Like most blokes, Paul prefers me make-up free and natural. It always makes me laugh that when we go out, girls (including myself back in the day) slap on the make-up, stuff our feet in high heels and wear the shortest skirts, and yet most blokes prefer us in simple clothes and with a natural face.

It's also easy to forget that I had been in the public eye since my teens. I'd had my fashion moments (good and bad!) for everyone to see splashed across magazine covers. I defy any girl not to have worn something horrendous at one point or another – the difference is that I had people picking up magazines in the dentist waiting room going 'What ON EARTH was she thinking?' In the past I've had press accuse me of having work done on my face (I haven't, by the way) because they say it has changed shape. That's what happens as we go from our teens into our twenties – our bone structure changes – but I also wear less make-up now. I go for far less of everything and much prefer the more natural look, so I do look quite different from when I was nineteen, but more on that later.

When I was pregnant, my hair was much darker and coarser, which meant I didn't have to worry about getting it coloured blonde and any chemicals harming the baby. I also had this really weird thing where the hair on my legs stopped growing as much. I googled the signs for having a boy and leg hair growth slowing down was one of them. I think that was when I decided it had to be a boy! It was funny because everyone told me I was mad to look at Google for things like that, but Billie had bad skin in the first few months she was pregnant with Nelly and when she googled it, she found out that it was a sign of having a girl, which was right too! Maybe there is something in these signs after all…

I was so busy focusing on becoming a mummy that the maintenance of my beauty routine became minimal. As the birth approached I tried to have things done that would save me time once the baby was here, like eyebrow tints, a fresh set of finger and toenail gels. I invested in a tinted moisturiser – little tricks that would help when I was short on time and sleep.

Things I noticed when I was pregnant:

- My skin was amazing, the best it had ever been. I know that was hormones but I also got into the habit of drinking masses of water, which helped. It was a great habit to get into for when I started breastfeeding.
- My nails were strong and grew lots.
- My hair was thick and shiny (I put this down to my diet as well as hormones).

- I didn't get any varicose veins or stretch marks – I think mainly as I soaked myself every day religiously in Bio-Oil. I slathered it on any opportunity I had, particularly on my boobs and belly. Poor Paul, I was covered in it for nine months!

Gearing up
for the Birth

Wanting to keep on working, and my determination not to let the pregnancy slow me down too much, meant that, at 29 weeks pregnant, I still had no birthing plan and no midwife, which worried everyone, including me. I'd had my 12 and 20 week scans at a private scan centre in Brentwood, but hadn't actually met a midwife yet. Most women when they're pregnant go to their GP, who refers them on to a midwife, and then you usually have your first booking-in appointment – where a midwife takes your bloods for testing, goes through you and your family's medical history, books you in for scans and answers any questions you may have – by 8 to 12 weeks. I got all that sorted 17 weeks later than most mums-to-be. Everyone was nagging me to get it done but you know what it's like with big stuff: you often put it off as it feels like too much hard work. It was such a big deal and for a few months I was also researching home versus hospital births, which meant I took my time in finding a midwife I wanted. Without getting all woo-woo, I did believe I was going to have an amazing birth. I told myself every day of my pregnancy that it would be great, that it would be smooth and we would both be fine: positive reinforcement. To me it was important that I kept positive vibes around me, and that's why I was so open to trying everything on offer that might help me cope with the birth and have the natural experience I so desperately wanted.

We made the decision to pay to have a private midwife and there were two good reasons for this that felt right for us. It took me so long to find a midwife and then, after the story of the pregnancy was leaked, we had an incident that I found difficult. After finally registering my pregnancy with my GP, we went to the hospital for a routine appointment. While we were in the waiting room, someone took a photo of us and then tried to sell a story. That was totally unacceptable for me – I wanted to protect my baby and our privacy, and I didn't want the hassle of worrying every time I went for a check-up that someone was taking my picture and trying to make money out of me. Someone actually put up on Twitter that I had been seen at Broomfield Hospital in the Mother and Baby Unit and one of my fans told me. I just thought, 'That's it, I have to do this privately so we can be in charge.'

Now I know there will be some readers out there thinking it's all right for her. And I get that: I know I was lucky to be in the position to afford to have someone come to my home and look after me and the baby, but I think if we hadn't had those negative experiences it would never have occurred to me. Any mum out there will know what it feels like to want to protect their baby. I just did what felt right for me and I am grateful I had the finances to do so. After having my pregnancy announcement hijacked, I wanted some control over such a big life event and that involved not being pictured on social media every time I went for a scan or a blood test.

At this point I still hadn't decided 100 per cent if I was going for a home or hospital birth and we had to pick a hospital to be linked to, so I chose Broomfields. I had been at Billie's and my friend Jeri's births there and was impressed with the first-class care they received, so Broomfields was my obvious choice when putting down a hospital. I didn't want to do the whole Portland thing – I think it is massively overpriced for what it is and it just wasn't for us; we didn't want to go down the glitzy route. I wanted to be near home, near my mum and Billie, and somewhere that felt familiar. To be honest, I felt there wasn't anything at the Portland we couldn't get at Broomfields: the rooms are massive, there is a birthing pool, a telly on the wall… Whatever I wanted was there right on my doorstep and it was like a home from home.

The second reason for going down the private midwife route was that, by this point, I was so late getting a midwife that I felt a bit desperate to get something proper in place. I had so many questions that I needed answering, so much buzzing round in my head, and I wanted someone to take charge. I needed to make up lost time and I knew I could do that better with a one-to-one person I could trust and talk to on a friendship level too. We were given a recommendation by a friend and didn't put too much thought into who we picked – I was told she was great and I just wanted to get going.

If I had to do it all over again, I would start looking into it all earlier than I did and maybe take a bit more time when choosing someone. When you are looking into private midwives, you always think a recommendation is bound to be the best, but choosing a midwife brings home the fact that every pregnancy and labour is different and what works for one person, even if you're friends, might not be right the right fit for you. Obviously, I know we were in a fortunate position and I know not everyone has that option.

We decided that if we were going to do it this way then we would go for the full birthing package, so we booked our midwife for the antenatal stage, the birth (which I was still researching) and two weeks post-natal. It didn't end up quite like that as I had the actual birth in hospital and then only had my midwife for one visit afterwards. Instead, I contacted Brentwood Midwifery and they came round a few times after the baby was born to do the post-care bit – they were amazing.

Home versus Hospital

When we first started thinking about where we wanted to have the baby, I didn't know a lot about home births. At that point I obviously only had the experience of friends and family who'd had their babies; all I knew about birth was what I'd seen of Billie having Nelly and my friend Jeri having hers – both of which were in hospital. Paul loves finding out about stuff and making sure that he is as well informed as he can be before he makes a decision, which is something that he has taught me. So when it came to us deciding how to do things, he encouraged me to read up on it all and when I did, I loved how having a home birth came across. I was nervous but that was only because I didn't know anyone else who'd had one and, like everything else surrounding first-time pregnancy, it was the unknown.

It sounded so relaxed and I fell in love with the idea of being in my own surroundings with all my own home comforts to hand. I could be in charge of how it all went, have there who I wanted (which was just as well as I wasn't planning on doing it by halves, I wanted four birthing partners: Paul, my mum, Gaynor and Billie), and just make it as stress-free as possible. I was going to rig the lounge with cameras to capture it all, as I wasn't sure that mum or Billie would be concentrating on getting all the best shots and I was determined to record every moment to look back on. The idea of being in my own space for such a life-changing event really appealed to me, as did the thought of being able to get straight into my own bed with fresh sheets and a cup of tea and biscuits – it sounded idyllic!

My feeling was that everything I needed was at home: it would be fully set up for the birth when we got a pool and if, God forbid, something did go wrong or not feel right (as happened with me) then you get transferred straight into hospital anyway. The more I read the more I was sure it was what I wanted. Looking back now I wouldn't change a thing about baby Paul's actual birth apart from the fact I would obviously have preferred him to have been delivered at home. But it was such a long day of labour that I don't know how I would have coped with all that time in a hospital. I hate hospitals – the smell, the stress – they bring back bad memories for me because of the Crohn's and the long stay I had while they tried to diagnose me. I didn't have a clue what was wrong with me and I was so scared. It was the worst time of my life and since I now associate hospital stays with being terrified, I didn't want to have that feeling when I was bringing our baby into the world. I had an idea in my head of a perfect, stress-free environment to welcome our baby into and I feel happy that I did all I could to make that happen. I would do it all over again next time too and I definitely plan to have my other babies at home if I can.

In the run-up to the birth, and to help form a proper idea of exactly what I wanted, I decided to do as many classes as I could and really find out what worked for me. While I was adamant from the start that I didn't want any pain relief, I knew I would need something to get through the labour! It was just a question of choosing the right thing, so I looked into hypnobirthing. Normally I would laugh at the idea of being told that something so obviously painful as childbirth could be done, drug-free, without the fear of pain. What appealed to me in the first instance was the idea that I could be in control and wouldn't just automatically give over all the say-so to the doctors or midwives looking after me. Childbirth, for me, was like anything else to do with my body: if I didn't understand it I would question it and find out more. Just because I didn't know anyone who'd given birth at home, it didn't mean I shouldn't. It was about being present in every sense – it was important to me that I felt fully aware of what was going on and that I could make the right choices at the right times for the baby – not be out of it on drugs unable to say what I wanted or how I felt.

When I went to my first hypnobirthing class (which you can see on *The Baby Diaries* – my mum found hilarious!) I was a bit sceptical. But it's like anything, isn't it? Until you have all the facts you can't have a proper opinion, and the more I found out about it, the more I liked the sound of it. My big tip here is to be as open-minded as you can, because these more 'alternative' ways of doing things will only work if you consider them properly and take them seriously. I knew I wanted to gather my own information but I also knew who the right people were to discuss things with. For example, there would be no point in recommending hypnobirthing to someone like Billie as she would probably laugh her way out of the class! She's just not the type to take it seriously, but if you are keen on alternative routes, make sure you explore as many different options as possible. The fact is that, even if none of them end up being right, you will be fully informed and feel happy that you looked into everything you could. There is so much out there and things have moved on from being on a bed, strapped to machines – there are so many different angles on birthing it's incredible.

The first thing I was told at my hypnobirthing session was that extreme pain doesn't have to be the only thing you associate with labour. If you are a first-time mum then hypnobirthing will help you release all your fear about giving birth and if you have had a baby before then you learn how to overcome previous traumatic births. It is all about the positives and the magic of birth, rather than any of the nightmare stories you might have been told; it's about creating your own story and that really appealed to me, rather than having people telling me how it would be.

Like many people, I associated hypnobirthing with hypnosis, and worried that it meant I would be in some kind of a trance and not fully aware of what was going on, but it isn't like that at all. Most people are still fully able to chat and engage in what is going on around them. In my case, I chose to have my eyes closed and not really talk that much, but that was just what worked for me at the time. However, I was always fully aware and fully in control of what was happening to me, and I didn't have any of the tension in my body that can stop the birthing muscles from doing what they need to do in order to get the baby out. The idea is to know what your body is doing and work with it, rather than against it, to allow the body to get on with the job at hand without the addition of stress, which can slow down the effectiveness of how the body works.

Given that I ended up relying on the breathing techniques and affirmations so much, I didn't give the build-up and preparation loads of time like you are supposed to. You have to attend the practice sessions regularly (ideally with your birthing partners so that they get the vibe of what is going on as well as being 100 per cent clear on what you want to happen once the labour actually progresses) but there is also loads of homework! I was a bit hit and miss with all the sessions as I was still working and Paul was mega busy at work too, but I did try and do the work at home. Me and Paul would sit on the sofa after dinner and go through all the affirmations but, to be honest, they'd send him straight to sleep. I decided to see that as a good thing – it showed they actually worked at relaxing you!

Hypnobirthing: the facts

- Hypnobirthing isn't pain relief, it is a method that has techniques to help you believe that your contractions are less painful. It is all about exploring a different attitude to the way we think and talk about labour and birth.

- It is a technique that is often believed to result in a shorter first-stage labour with less intense pain – the obvious end result of that would be a shorter stay in hospital and a quicker recovery.
- It is believed that you will experience less fear and anxiety after the birth of your baby and feel more in control, even though you have been through a physical ordeal and your whole world has changed in an instant.
- The classes are often spread out over five to eight weekly sessions depending on where you live and what your local centre is like.
- Most classes start around week 30–32, which gives you plenty of time to practise.
- In the classes you will learn about key positions for labour and birth (e.g., staying upright as much as possible can help shorten the labour), deep relaxation and self-hypnosis – methods that help you stay alert but also shut out the world and focus on your breathing to relax your body.
- The relaxation breathing will help you release the hormone oxytocin, which eases labour.

I also did some pregnancy yoga as it's a great way to prepare the body for labour by stretching muscles and strengthening the body, and brilliant for helping you stay calm and focused. I promised myself that I would keep up the yoga once the baby was here and find us some mother and baby classes, but I just haven't had the time.

Pregnancy yoga

- I found that antenatal yoga really helped to keep me toned during pregnancy. It was also great for stretching my hip and abdominal core muscles in preparation for labour.

- Yoga builds muscle tone and increases flexibility, which helps with the aches and pains as you get bigger and start to carry more weight. It is also fantastic for getting your body back after you've had the baby as the muscles have great memory.

- A bit like hypnobirthing, antenatal yoga helps you trust that your body will open up and do what it needs to during labour. When we are stressed and scared our muscles tense up. Working on breathing and muscle relaxation will let you do what your body instinctively needs to do during birth. At the end of the day, all this helps make the process as natural as possible.

- Going to the classes allows you to have an hour off your feet and give you time to think about your baby and what life will be like once he or she is here. I found it was quiet time for just me and the baby in the middle of a hectic working week and I loved it.

- Yoga is brilliant for helping with all the aches and pains that pregnancy brings – especially lower back pain and shortness of breath at the very end when the baby is pressing on everything.

- Keeping the muscles stretched keeps the blood moving round your body, and all the controlled breathing helps with the oxygen supply to the baby and the placenta.

Reflexology

In truth, I'm not sure how much this helped me during the actual birth. I went mainly because it just really relaxed me and allowed me to sit down for half an hour! At the point I went in my pregnancy I was about seven to eight months gone, so the bump was big and it was obviously more weight to carry than I was used to. It was just nice to take the weight off and have my feet rubbed! It was so lovely at the end of the pregnancy to feel pampered when I felt so physically uncomfortable and unlike myself – it was like having a full body massage on my feet.

On a more serious side, it was explained to me that reflexology is an ancient form of healing and the idea is to have regular sessions throughout your pregnancy to help achieve a calmer birth and produce babies who are more settled, as they will have benefited from the reflexology too. It is claimed that reflexology babies breastfeed better and that women who have a Caesarean recover quicker.

With all the hormones released in the body during pregnancy (the foetus releases some and the mother does too – we mainly release relaxin, which is an ovarian hormone that softens the pelvic muscles in preparation for birth) it is no wonder our hormones (and moods!) can be all over the place. Such dramatic changes can be overwhelming and cause imbalances in pregnant women. Reflexology clears these imbalances in our energy channels, which can become blocked due to these sudden changes.

What is reflexology?

- It is around 5,000 years old and sometimes called 'zonal therapy' as the body is divided into specific zones with matching reflex points.

- When these points and zones are stimulated, a message is sent to the spine and central nervous system, and from that point a signal is sent to the brain and other organs.

- A typical session will involve applying pressure, stretching and movement using specific techniques with a thumb and finger combination. This combination will be used on the reflex points that can be found in feet, lower legs, hands, face and ears.

- The idea is that reflexology encourages the body to relax, it improves circulation, stimulates the organs and helps the body to naturally heal.

- The main aim is to allow the body, mind and soul to work together as smoothly as possible.

- It can also help women towards the end of their pregnancy if their baby is in the breech position and needs to be encouraged to turn on his or her own, without medical intervention.

- Women who are trying to get pregnant often say that reflexology helps them, mainly as it calms you down and puts you in a happy, calm place, allowing the body to relax into conceiving.

Babymoons and Baby Showers

When I was seven months pregnant, me and Paul took our last trip as a couple on our own, and we decided to make it one to remember. Looking back, like most practical things it seems, I did leave it a bit late to travel and I reckon we just about got away with it. I was 30 weeks pregnant when we flew to the Maldives at the beginning of November and it was the best holiday of my life.

We had always intended to go away – we thought it was important to cement our relationship with some uninterrupted couple time together before we became three. The trip ended up happening just after our one-year anniversary and so felt like the perfect time, even though so much had happened that it felt much longer than twelve months, given I had been pregnant for seven of them! I was fine getting the main flight out there, even though it was quite long, although I did get a bit swollen. The problem started when we landed and had to get transferred on to a seaplane to get to our island. They almost didn't let me on as they said I was too pregnant and they couldn't risk taking me in case I went into early labour. We very nearly had to come up with a plan B and find somewhere else to fly to that didn't involve sea planes to remote islands (Dubai was the likely destination), but in the end they relented and whisked us away for the most idyllic stay. Thank God as I might just have had a hormonal cry at that point – I couldn't wait to get to our magical place and relax.

We had a private beach villa in the five-star Dusit Thani hotel – it had its own luxury pool and beach-side location too – we were truly spoilt! Paul was so romantic too – he organised a beautiful, private dinner on our own beach and had sorted all the small details like candles and flowers. He said some lovely things about how much he loved me and what a great mum he thought I would be, and we made some perfect memories as a couple before we became a proper little family. Obviously, I know it is unusual to jet off to the Maldives, but if you can get away, even just for the weekend, you should. I think that taking time where it is just the two of you, to celebrate each other as well as discussing what is to come, it is well worth it – we still talk about it all the time.

Once we got back from getting some winter sun and I had looked into all the various ways that might help me get the baby out, I decided to turn my attention to one last celebration before the baby arrived and mark the pregnancy with a baby shower to end all showers…

Baby shower

It should be obvious to anyone who knows anything about me that there was no way I could be pregnant and not have a full-on glam baby shower! It was funny really – I think I was so low-key during my pregnancy and loved staying indoors just chilling on the sofa, but the shower really mattered to me as a chance to get together with my nearest and dearest. It was such a special time to be treasured before the baby came, and I was running around taking loads of photos of everyone and making new memories. I was so near the end of the pregnancy, which meant I was very hormonal and feeling quite sentimental about how much everyone meant to me and how much our baby would be loved.

Because it was December it felt so festive, with Christmas decorations everywhere and beautiful trees laden with tinsel and lights in every corner of the two rooms we had hired at Greenwoods Hotel & Spa – a dramatic fireplace with big silver baubles and garlands set the whole thing off to make it look like a winter wonderland, it was amazing. I think this is where some of my nesting mania set in – I was 36 weeks pregnant and obsessed with everything being perfect. There were giant balloons, and an amazing gold cake topped with a gold pram, with gold cupcakes and hearts all around it and 'Baby Knightley' iced on them. I planned everything down to the final point but my baby brain meant I forgot basics like booking a room for everyone to get ready in, which meant that we had to get changed and do our make-up in the toilets – that didn't go down well! But what made it so special was the guest list: my mum, Billie, Nelly, my nanny Liz, Gaynor and all my friends and old crew from my teenage years. It was such a special day.

I felt great, if a bit heavy and slow. The chat was obviously about babies and pregnancy, and Luisa was telling me how great hypnobirthing was. (She used it for both her births and seemed to give birth in an hour each time – shame it wasn't the same for me!) By then, I had explored everything that was available to me because I wanted to have as much knowledge as possible. The shower felt a bit like a low-key wedding – there was a photo booth, sandwiches, sausage rolls, chicken dippers, brownies and other desserts.

I couldn't find anything I wanted to wear and so picked the dress at the last minute. It was quite glitzy and shimmery – perfect for the festive season – from Bec & Bridge. It wasn't actually a maternity dress so I just got a larger size and took in the shoulders so that it fitted perfectly. I had strappy heels on for most of the party but went barefoot for the last hour as everything was so swollen – a real Kim K moment! Rather unglamorously, I also got a sharp pain under my ribs just as the party was about to start – it really hurt and I was a bit worried there might be something wrong with the baby so I called the midwife who duly told me it was trapped wind!

It was magical but I was also very emotional and overwhelmed by all the love in the room; it made me feel so special and loved just before the big day. When Billie made a lovely speech about how happy she was for me and what great parents me and Paul would make it finished me off and I burst into floods of tears. Billie wasn't much better – she was so nervous about standing up and speaking that she had to go outside and practise, not that she got much chance to collect her thoughts with Nelly running around!

It was a lovely way for us all to celebrate this big milestone and it was just perfect. I definitely recommend gathering your nearest and dearest round you and marking the moment somehow – it doesn't have to be as full-on as mine. But it is a lovely way to make memories if you are starting a baby box of mementos. More importantly, it is probably also the last chance you will get to dress up and finish a whole conversation with anyone for at least four months!

Tips for the end of the pregnancy:

- You can often get carried away at the start, taking every vitamin on offer and taking on board all the advice you are given – but nine months is a long time and carrying on the good intentions is hard. Try to only start things you feel you can keep up until the very last bit.

- Improvise and take the help you can, even with the small stuff. Paul had to shave my legs towards the end, as I couldn't reach!

- Take a last break before you become parents if you can – it will really help you to reconnect and stay strong during those first sleep-deprived months.

- SLEEP. Just sleep all the time, whenever you can. It will be a long time before you get any once your baby is here!

- Get lashes and eyebrows tinted – it will help with the fact you won't have time to put on make-up once the baby arrives.

- Batch cook and freeze meals – you will be so glad you did when you are sleep-deprived and starving.

- Keep a pad and pen in your handbag. You will forget *everything* towards the end!

Baby Shopping

I surprised myself with my 'less is more' approach to this area of preparation as it is most unlike me! But I really did keep it to a minimum. Make lots of lists would be my main advice, and remember that no stage in a baby's first year or two lasts for very long, so be logical. For example, don't worry about buying a toddler pram when you're still pregnant – think about what you need now as you can buy as you go.

What you really need

- Vests and babygrows, which are also called babysuits and sleep-suits in shops. You always need baby vests and babygrows. Me and Paul were determined to put the baby in fresh white clothes, whatever the sex, I just liked the clean and unfussy feel of white. Start with 7–10 newborn-size vests and see how you go.
- Muslins are essential – buy tons of them. I promise you can never have enough.

- Stock up on basics and don't worry about outfits – when they are tiny you don't need complicated dungarees or dresses with tights and hundreds of poppers. Make life easy for yourself because there will be a LOT of nappy changing! I stocked up on 7–10 plain newborn sleepsuits.

- Two cardigans. Babies can't regulate their temperature in the way that older children and adults can, so it's best to dress your newborn in layers, to put on and take off depending on the temperature.

- Socks, hats, dribble bibs, scratch mitts and booties (especially in winter as their little feet are always cold).

- Don't make any big decisions about feeding or sleeping until he or she is here: you just never know how you will feel. I bought a bottle steriliser and a SnuzPod (a crib which attaches to the side of your bed) and I ended up breastfeeding on demand and co-sleeping! You just won't know until the baby arrives and you often do the opposite of what you think you will. The last thing you need is a house full of equipment you're not using – there will be enough chaos, believe me!

- A Moses basket for downstairs as well as one upstairs will be a big help, so that you can keep the baby nearby during the day and you don't have to keep running up and down the stairs to check on him.

- Two changing mats – one for upstairs and night-time nappy changing, and one for downstairs during the day. It will be a lifesaver on your legs!

- Up to four swaddling blankets.
- A car seat – essential for getting the baby home as the hospital will not let you leave without one – and a sun protector for use in the car if it is summer.
- Changing bag.
- A baby bath and a thermometer for testing the water and making sure it isn't too hot or cold.
- Up to four hooded towels.
- A baby sling. It's a great way for the dad to feel close to the baby too and means you can be hands-free when you're out and about – I found it essential for supermarket shopping in the early days.
- Breast pads and sanitary towels for you, as well as tops with easy access to your boobs for breastfeeding, if that's what you are going to do.
- Nursing bras are also a must – they aren't sexy but they are essential!

The Birth

When I was younger, I always thought I would be full of drama when it came to the whole giving-birth thing – you know, like you see in the films with all the screaming. I tell Paul all the time that he got off lightly (I did eventually get a 'push present', even if I did have to wait six months...)! I was super calm throughout my 22-hour labour, even though I had a back-to-back birth – where the baby's back is against your back, which can make labour more difficult – with only a bit of gas and air. I also had cameras capturing the moment in the knowledge it would be shown on ITV at a later date, which isn't something I would recommend (it was certainly the only time I have been on TV and not thought about a make-up artist!). Hypnobirthing is amazing because, at heart, it is all about giving you control at a time when you feel like you have none. It was the best thing for me, and I know I will do it for every birth, not least as it gave me such a sense of calm at a time when it would have been easy to feel stressed and overwhelmed.

Like most first-time mums, I thought I knew how it would be: we hired a huge birthing pool (which we didn't have a chance to set up before I went into labour as the baby was so early), I had nice soft music playing, *Friends* on the TV in the background, and I had my eyes closed and concentrated on my hypno-breathing – it was like a TV advert. But then my temperature spiked and we were rushed to hospital, with a dehydrated me in the passenger seat of our car, in agony, but just calmly breathing through the pain, eyes shut, waiting to meet my baby.

The day of the birth started off really normally, not least because as far as I was concerned, we were still far away from the big day. With that in mind we went to Leeds to spend Christmas with Paul's family and I wasn't concerned about going into labour. I still had over two weeks until my due date and I fully expected to go over that so, in my head, I had another month. It was the first Christmas I had ever spent away from my family, which felt strange. I guess that's what happens when you get into a relationship; you have to take turns! I felt absolutely fine and it never occurred to me that I should stay close to home. We got to Leeds and I was looked after and cooked for. It was lovely to put my feet up.

Everyone talks about that final burst of energy – some women clean their house from top to toe – and I used my burst to go for a long walk. After days inside eating loads of food and watching Christmas TV with my feet up, I needed to get out and let off some steam. I needed fresh air, so I joined everyone on the walk to Bolton Abbey, near Skipton, which took four hours! It was the maddest walk – at times it was so steep that Paul had to push me up from behind and someone else would have to pull me from the front. How I did that walk I will never know, because everyone else struggled and I powered on through. I felt great, though, like I could take on the world. That night, in the car on the journey home to Essex, I was laid out on the back seat, Paul and Gaynor in the front, and I started to feel some twinges. Nothing major, and given the amount I had eaten and the long walk, it was no surprise really that I felt a bit weird, like I'd overdone it.

When we got to Gaynor's it was quite late and I told them I'd had these pains all the way home. It didn't cross my mind that I could be in labour, especially as Billie went over ten days. I thought I'd go right over and, with the two weeks I already had to go, to my mind that made it ages away. I told Paul and he was grinning at me but I could tell that he was really nervous – we both were.

He told me to ring the midwife and she advised me to see how I got on for an hour or so and call back if anything changed. I went to sit on the toilet and had a show – the mucus plug that comes away from your cervix in early labour – in my pyjama bottoms, so called her back just as the pain started to become a bit more full-on. She said it sounded like early labour but that I must get as much rest as I could, as it would probably be a long road ahead. So I went upstairs to lie down on Paul's bed for a few hours till 4am, when I woke up to the pain coming thick and fast. We got in the car to get back to my house and set up the birthing pool, and from getting in the car to arriving at mine, the pain went off the scale. It took 30 minutes for everything to step up 100 gears. I didn't even have a hospital bag packed, but we were very calm.

I called my mum and Billie in the car on the way back home even though it was early in the morning because, as I've mentioned before, I was doing it in totally OTT style and having four birthing partners: Mum, Billie, Paul and Gaynor. We got home at about 6am and nothing was ready – we weren't prepared for this at all! The midwife was waiting on our driveway and the first thing I did when I got in was change my outfit into something comfy. I remember being in the dressing room with Billie, looking at all my clothes and worrying about how pale I looked! I didn't have a scrap of make-up on and I remember reaching for the eyeliner and trying to put it on using the small mirror in there. I just needed something to make me feel like me. I had asked Billie to photograph and film everything and, although it sounds mental to some, I wanted to look and feel nice. I was trying so hard to keep my hand steady but I only managed to do one eye until a contraction came. So there I was, liquid eyeliner in hand, bending over my dressing room table, breathing through the pain, one eye done, one eye to do – it was hilarious. Billie looked at me and said, 'Come on, Sam, just leave that!'

Some of her footage made it on to the show *The Baby Diaries*. Having a camera around while you're having your contractions is not something I would advise – thinking the footage being taken as you breathe through a contraction will be seen on national TV doesn't really help with the pain. You can actually see on the show that I didn't really talk at all through the contractions, which surprised my mum! Whenever a contraction came, there was no swearing, no shouting, no panicking, I was just humming my way through it.

Date night for me and Paul, not long before I found out I was pregnant.

Smart in my Christmas Day stripy onesie, little did I know I was about to pop early!

Our beautiful babymoon (and me in the only bikini that fitted me!)

Having a special moment with Gaynor at my gorgeous baby shower.

Boxing Day slump – resting up before the long walk that ended in contractions!

Fully submerged in the pool and in full swing, 10 hours of labour down and no idea I was only halfway!

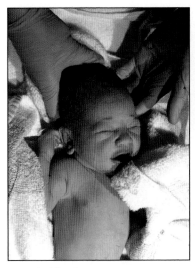

Seconds old and so precious.

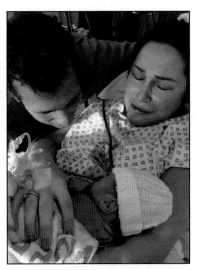

Tears of exhaustion and utter joy – nothing can prepare you for the first time you meet your baby.

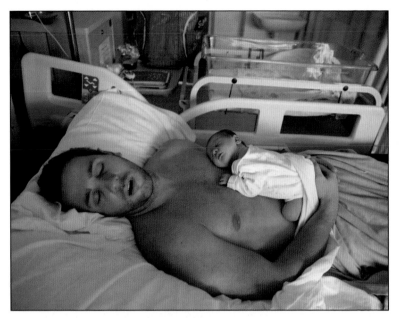

Paul clearly exhausted after my long labour!

Big Paul sleeping through our first family selfie.

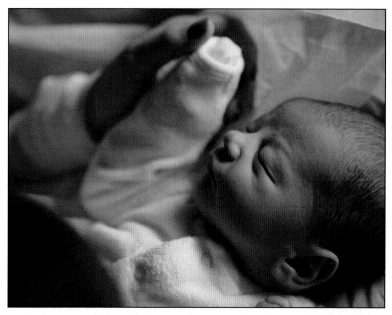

The most perfect little face I looked at for hours – I can still remember how silky soft his skin was.

Auntie Billie getting in her first cuddle, she quickly became known as the 'baby hogger'!

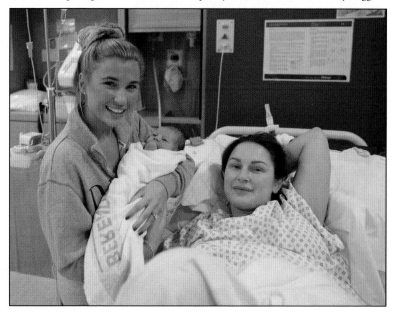

Our favourite
breastfeeding position
– rugby ball hold.

Then there were three
– my perfect family.

Five generations – baby Paul meets his great, great nanny Marot and great nanny Liz.

Fresh out of the jungle – baby Paul meets Ferne.

All clean and fresh in his bathrobe.

I had been practising my yoga and breathing techniques, and was in and out of the pool. I had one hypnobirthing soundtrack that I got them to play over and over again – it was like whale music and affirmations all rolled into one – but I found it so soothing. I ended up knowing when it was coming to an end and I would say, 'Again, again,' before it had even finished. Imagine it – one song for 22 hours. It drove everyone totally mad!

I was completely in the zone the whole time and the vibe was lovely. At one point Billie went back to her house, which is only a mile away, to get me a fan as I was so hot. Even though I was doing my best to stay calm and relaxed, the pain in my lower back was excruciating. My mum was rubbing my back all day and I wouldn't let her stop – it's a miracle she didn't do herself an injury. We didn't find out until I went to hospital that I was having a back-to-back labour (where the baby is facing towards your stomach rather than your spine.) Mums out there who have had back-to-back labours will know exactly what I'm talking about – it hurts so much because the baby is pressing down on all your nerves. It also means that, because of the angle, the baby isn't always pressing down on the right points of the cervix to ensure a speedy and complete dilation – which can mean a longer labour.

I was also in the shower a lot and telling Paul to direct the boiling hot water right on my lower back; Paul said at the time he was terrified he was going to scald me! The water was so hot that he almost burned his hand on the showerhead. It was such a relief though and the only thing that took the edge off the pain. But

MY BABY AND ME

of course, looking back, I can see that was why my temperature went sky high and that worried the midwife because it's obviously dangerous. So that, combined with the fact my contractions had slowed down, meant that she wanted to get me transferred to Broomfields Hospital for the actual delivery.

But before all that it was a long day of labouring, and going through the process at home was peaceful and relaxing. I felt in control in my own space and like I knew what was happening without lots of doctors going in and out, whispering in corners and holding clipboards. I was so clear about how I wanted to have my baby but at the same time we didn't want to do anything at all that would risk his, or my, safety. Unfortunately you can make all the plans in the world, but it just depends how it goes on the day and you can never know what's going to happen. No amount of preparation can guarantee that you get the labour you want, so I was determined to go with the flow and not get uptight.

There was a point in the birthing pool when my midwife told me I had to get up and move around as my contractions were slowing right down and that would prolong, if not stop, everything. Paul was great and walked me around the kitchen and held me up because we had to keep everything moving so the baby didn't get too comfortable in there. I managed until 8pm before I had my first bit of gas and air, but then things started to get a bit tricky because everything really slowed right down. I was so relaxed, it was almost like the contractions all stopped but the problem was that my temperature went sky high. When it goes too high you are prone to infection and it can indicate that something is wrong, so the midwife made the decision for me to be transferred to hospital. We left home at around 11pm, about 18 hours after the labour started and 4 hours from the end. We were upset but we knew the priority had to be getting the baby out safely and quickly. I told myself that it didn't matter that the plan had changed; it was the outcome that I needed to stay focussed on now.

Billie quickly packed a bag as we hadn't even done that – she threw in some babygrows, two tracksuits, a toothbrush, my camera, nappies and toiletries. Deep down I was gutted – I felt like I had come so far and I really wanted to have the baby at home. That's why Paul took so much time and asked so many questions – we both really wanted to see it through in our calm and chilled home environment. I had planned this beautiful home birth and suddenly I couldn't have it. But the midwife told me that I was 8cm dilated by this point so it had to be a quick decision – hospital was what we had to do and we were calm and just got on with the job in hand.

The hospital was half an hour away by car and Paul drove me there, with Gaynor in the back. She had her arms around me and I sat in the front passenger seat with my eyes closed, just concentrating on staying calm and keeping my breathing regular. I had my eyes closed for most of the day actually, as it was something that really helped me keep in the right zone and calm. Mum and Billie followed behind us in the car and the midwife came in her car too – this long convoy on the way to the hospital. I was determined to stay relaxed: I was fine, the baby was fine, and we needed to take each step as it came and not make it a drama. I didn't really worry about giving birth in the car either as, typically, as soon as I got in the car the contractions slowed right down and I only had four in total on the thirty-minute drive.

We got to hospital and they rushed me straight in. The rules were only two birthing partners as it was now classed as an emergency. Mum said, 'Look, you know obviously I want to be there but I understand if you want your sister instead.'

I looked at her and said, 'No, I want you, Mummy.'

Within ten minutes of arrival they told me that I was having a back-to-back labour and straight away they offer you an epidural and morphine. I remember clearly saying that I didn't want any of that – I had come this far without and I was determined to do it as naturally as possible. They couldn't believe I had gone so far with absolutely nothing – the first bit of gas and air I'd had was at the house at 8pm, 3 hours before I got into hospital, 15 hours after I went into labour. We only had one small canister at home and so I had to ration myself at the house – once I got to hospital and had it on tap, I really appreciated it!

They immediately gave me oxytocin to speed up my contractions and examined me. Typically, as soon as we got there my temperature had gone back to normal – it was most definitely all the scalding shower water! I was dehydrated so they put me on a drip to get fluids into me – I hadn't wanted to eat or drink a thing since I first went into labour so my body needed fuel. Everyone had tried to get me to sip water but I couldn't stand it, and Mum and Paul tried to feed me Jelly Babies for sugar and energy but I spat them straight out!

My contractions had been about five minutes apart but now they were suddenly every two minutes. In fact I'm not sure they every really stopped in between – it didn't feel like it to me anyway! It was a bit confusing at the hospital as the midwife had told me at home that I was a certain amount dilated, and then when I got to hospital they told me something completely different, that I was less than I thought. At the house she had told me I was almost ready to push, which was why we were so disappointed to have to go to the hospital when we were so close. But that's the way it was so I just had to get on with it. Once I had made it clear I didn't want any actual pain relief, my blood pressure got high and the hospital immediately took charge.

It turned out that I had an anterior cervical lip – this is when part of the cervix doesn't fully dilate with the rest. In my case, the back of the cervix was fully dilated at 10cm and the front was only 9.5cm. The bit that isn't fully dilated often gets swollen and slows down the progress from stage one to two and then also obstructs the baby being pushed out. All very complicated and technical but, basically, every time I thought I was on my way to pushing him out, he was going back in! Sometimes this condition can trick the body so you are pushing away, believing you are fully dilated, but you are not and so the pushing urge comes to nothing, as you aren't really ready to deliver.

The doctor came in and I knew that was bad news – I felt like he was eyeing me up for a C-section. I was told that my blood pressure was high and I absolutely had to push this baby out now or it would be a C-section. I remember Paul coming down to me, putting his face right next to mine and saying, 'Babe, you can do this. You have to do this now.'

I was beyond exhausted, with a tiredness I can't describe, but the body is the most amazing thing; you can just find energy from somewhere when you are determined enough, and I was *so* determined I would push this baby out. It's like nothing you can explain, this animal instinct: I was going to push this baby out whatever it took!

The doctor had to push the lip to one side using his fingers, which made more space for the baby to come out. You always think you are going to feel really funny about being naked in front of people and that having them prodding around down there will feel really awful, but by that time I couldn't have cared less what was going on!

They told me that on the next contraction they wanted me to push as hard as I could, through my bum, like I was having a poo. That was my first go but I knew that wasn't going to cut it! I looked back at the end of the labour and realised that first push wasn't going to get us anywhere! God knows where I found the strength from but it was almost like the maternal instinct was kicking in before he had even been born; I knew I had to get him out safely and I was going to do anything to make that happen.

Paul was up my end – I had said at the start that I didn't want him down at the business end. My mum was down there and I didn't mind that – she wasn't going to be put off! At the point of pushing though, again, I didn't care who saw what and it wouldn't have mattered if Paul had wanted to get involved with what was going on down there. Paul didn't want to, though. He said that I'd always been clear I didn't want that and he wanted to respect my wishes, even if I had changed my mind in the heat of the moment. (I think a bit of him was probably quite relived about that conversation!)

He was up with me and he had both his arms round me, facing me and I was holding him round the neck and pushing. I was squeezing him so hard, I don't know how I didn't strangle him! That last bit of pushing wasn't too bad on the pain scale, as the worst had been the back pain. I just went for it and pushed the baby out in 45 minutes, holding on to Paul the whole time.

Poor Billie and Gaynor were pacing around in the waiting room and I felt gutted they couldn't see baby Paul being born. Billie was texting Mum for updates about what was going on but she was a bit busy with the task at hand! Paul was amazing during the actual pushing stage – he never left my side and encouraged me all the way through.

When they said at 3.03am 'It's a boy' I wasn't remotely surprised. I knew from day one it was a boy and I called the bump 'he' from the start. Everyone at the baby shower was convinced it was a girl but I just had an instinct that I was having a boy – I think me and Paul both did.

I was a bit hysterical when he was born. I had tried for so long to keep calm and stay in the zone, but he came out and they put him straight on to my chest and we all had a big cuddle and were all crying – I couldn't keep my tears in. Paul says he remembers hearing me say to baby Paul, 'Mummy's here.'

It was like my whole body went into shock, it was an amazing feeling because all the pain had gone and all I felt was pure joy. I started crying and I didn't stop really for six weeks. Obviously I knew birth was emotional because I was there for Nelly's, but nothing prepared me for when it was my turn. I still can't explain it – it overwhelms you in every way. That moment when they put him straight on to my chest, skin on skin, it was the most amazing feeling in the world and I will remember it forever. Paul cut the cord and then Billie and Gaynor came to meet him.

We named him Paul after his dad. It's a family tradition and baby Paul's middle name is Tony after his uncle Tony, Paul's brother. He weighed 6lb 15oz and he was perfect. Our life as a family of three had started and I couldn't have been happier.

Birth tips

- Pick your birthing partners and give them clear jobs.
- Make sure everyone in the room knows about your ideal birthing plan scenario – you will be too distracted by the pain and what's going on to always communicate what you want.
- Be clear about pain relief and don't be pressured either way – it's your birth and, as long as neither of you are in danger, do it your way.
- Be open to everything and don't make your mind up too early on. I tried yoga, hypnobirthing, reflexology on my feet – anything that was offered.

- Have someone calm taking notes – you get different viewpoints and there are lots of examinations. You need someone on the ball listening to what is being said.
- Don't keep telling a labouring woman to 'push' as if we don't know how to get the baby out. We know, we are trying, believe me.
- Blokes: don't fall asleep while rubbing the back of a woman in labour – that isn't okay.
- Get someone to film and take pictures – once you get over the actual birth and you look back a few months afterwards, it will be impossible to believe your baby was ever that tiny. It's beautiful to have those keepsakes.

Top Tip – Pack a
Hospital Bag Early!

I wasn't remotely ready when I went into labour early and, though Billie did a brilliant job of getting me a bag sorted as we were leaving to go to the hospital, it's a good idea to get yourself a bag packed early just in case. I was lucky that I only had to stay in for one night, but if things don't go to plan you might be in there for longer, so make sure you have everything you might need for a few nights.

Clothes for you

- Tracksuits – these will be comfy if you are in for a few days and you don't want to be in your PJs when visitors come.
- Pyjamas/comfies – I packed button down ones to help with the breastfeeding access.
- T-shirts – good for when you are sitting up in bed under the covers as you don't need to wear trousers, which is much more comfortable.
- Socks.

- Maternity knickers.
- Maternity bras.

Your wash bag

- Facial wash.
- Shower gel – unperfumed is best as your body will probably be sensitive after labour.
- Day and night moisturiser.
- Toothbrush and toothpaste.
- Flannel.
- Shampoo and conditioner.
- LOTS of maternity pads – these are essential!
- Hairbrush – but believe me, you won't have time to use a hairdryer!
- Lavender bath oil – this might be wishful thinking, but worth packing it in case you get time for a relaxing bath!
- Top tip: don't bother with make-up or anything like tweezers or hair tongs.

Extras

- Your birth plan – it is always worth having multiple copies of this just in case.
- A water bottle – though I didn't want water during labour, it is a good idea to drink it if you can, as dehydration can interfere with the labour.
- Face spray – to cool you down.

- Mini fan.
- Magazines – people will probably bring them (and let's face it, there will be no time to read them!) but worth packing just in case.
- Phone charger and phone/tablet.

For the baby

- Four white babygrows, which are the all-in-ones with feet and reversible hand mitts to stop the baby from scratching itself and are also called sleepsuits.
- Four white vests (also called bodysuits) with long sleeves.
- Four white vests (bodysuits) without sleeves.
- Don't bother with a 'going home outfit' – it will just be a white babygrow!
- A blanket or shawl to wrap around the baby in his or her car seat.
- If it's winter you might need a snowsuit, which is like an all-in-one coat.
- One pack of newborn nappies – make sure you get the right size!
- One bag of cotton wool.

Whatever you plan for the birth of your baby, and whatever happens during labour, just think how wonderful it will be, after all those months of waiting, to hold your little one in your arms for the first time; to smell their special baby smell, to marvel at their perfect little fingers and toes, and to feel their body snuggle into yours. It is such a lovely time of discovery, try to treasure every second of it.

Home Time

It is definitely true what they say about the body blocking out the pain of birth – let's face it, the human race would have died out otherwise! In the immediate few days afterwards it was all a blur and a lot of the detail is pretty hazy.

There are key things that I remember – mainly Paul in the kitchen blowing up the pool, which took forever. I remember the pain was all in my lower back and it was excruciating. I couldn't think about what was going on anywhere else in my body, my back was breaking – the contractions would come in big surges and I thought they were going to knock me off my feet.

When I had Crohn's disease and was in the middle of violent flare-ups, I would have these indescribable pains in my lower stomach – it's like a knife in your stomach being twisted and I remember thinking at that time, this must be like having contractions. With those pains I was doubled over and couldn't imagine worse agony – but labour was a whole different ball game. But then, as soon as he was born, all the labour memories drifted out of my mind and instead my brain became occupied by all-consuming love for my baby, as well as delirious exhaustion!

They say it is completely natural to get the baby blues after giving birth, but my only blues centred around being in hospital. I felt so down because I just wanted to get home and be around my own things, be back with Paul and get baby Paul safely indoors and all cosy. Don't get me wrong, the hospital staff were brilliant and looked after us so well, but they wouldn't let Paul stay with me and I hated him having to go home.

They told him to go home to bed and make the most of all the rest he could get before we came back to the house but he didn't want to leave us. He was supposed to leave at 9pm but stayed until 12.30am. In the end the nurse said to him, 'I've been very lenient. I've asked four times and if you stay then I have to let all the other dads stay too.'

I thought that was fair enough so Paul left and I was lying there crying my eyes out with a brand-new baby. I couldn't sleep and neither did Paul.

It was also around this time that I started to get to grips with breastfeeding – in fact, the first thing the midwives do straight after the birth is encourage you to feed. I will talk about this in more detail later on in the book, but as how to feed your baby is one of the first important decisions you will make, I thought it would be helpful to mention it here. When they put baby Paul on my chest, he immediately started to look around for food and with a bit of manoeuvring he latched on immediately. In those early days they do fall off and on the boob, and you realise that there is a real knack to it; they don't just always latch on straight away and stay there sucking away happily – it doesn't work like that! They have to get to grips with it and it's all about the angle of the baby and the boob – it's a lot to take in when you have just pushed out a baby! I remember sitting in the hospital bed, on my own, with this new baby and a breastfeeding sheet where I had to write down all the times of the feeds and which boob I had last used and I felt overwhelmed – I just wanted to be at home with my family.

Paul had gone home, tidied up and put the pool away, and then we FaceTimed each other. Eventually, after a long night, I called him at 9am the next morning to say that he could pick me up and he arrived with the car seat in record speed! I waited for him to get to my room so that I could have my shower knowing that he was watching baby Paul. That was another reason I was so desperate to get home – I didn't like the thought of being around people who weren't friends and family. Having baby Paul brought all my emotions to the surface and, even though the staff had been amazing and looked after us so well, I couldn't help but see danger everywhere! I didn't like strangers in and out of the room, looking at baby Paul and not really knowing who was doing what. I knew it was necessary but I was looking forward to some calm in my own bed.

I had my shower in record time, which was my first taste of what it would be like from then on – having to shower in under five minutes and be dressed and ready to deal with baby Paul. Gone were the days of leisurely face packs and lovely stay-in hair-conditioning treatments! I got myself ready and immediately sorted out baby Paul. It was a weird feeling, but at the same time it felt totally natural if that makes sense? Like I had been doing it forever, while also being terrified at how tiny he was. I remember dressing baby Paul in his fresh white babygrow, wrapping him up in his blanket and snowsuit, and putting him in his car seat. We had the usual mucking about with the car seat straps, making sure they were the right length and he was secure, while checking they also weren't too tight and going to crush him!

Once we were all ready we had loads of paperwork to fill in and eventually left at midday. Getting home was the best feeling in the world – the tears then were of absolute joy.

'Let Me Know
When I Can Pop
Round for a Cuddle...'

We brought baby Paul home on 31st December 2015, which is also my birthday. The idea that we could ration out our visitors was laughable: it was Christmas, we'd had a baby, it was my birthday and everyone wanted to celebrate the New Year! The house was brimming with people wanting a cuddle, asking to hear the birth story over and over again, bringing me presents – the phone didn't stop and it was chaos. I really don't mean to sound miserable or ungrateful, but all I wanted was to sleep! I hadn't slept a wink in the hospital, we'd got home and had to settle in, and then the next day everyone was round with cards and presents. Bless my mum, she came round with a birthday cake but I could barely keep my eyes open long enough for everyone to sing and for me to blow out the candles! Friends like Ferne came round and cooked us meals, and Mum and Gaynor came with dinners and extras that we could freeze, which was an amazing help. Knowing that we were going to be fed was one of the main things that got us through the early days.

I was utterly exhausted and feeling vulnerable as I was determined to get to grips with breastfeeding. I suppose I just wanted a calm and clean environment, and I wanted me and baby Paul to have rest and recover from the birth.

'You look absolutely glowing,' they all said.

Believe me, for the first few days there was no glamour. I was wearing nipple pads and had my boobs hanging out of my bra! I barely left the house for six weeks, felt a bit emotional, and my boobs were massive, SO massive. It was a world away from my previous life and I was elated and terrified in equal measure.

There was this little scrap – he needed me and everything else went out of the window, including all the rules I thought I would follow once he was here. I bought every sleep contraption under the sun – I mean everything – and where did baby Paul sleep? Literally on me in the bed. Mainly because I wanted him close and still do – we co-slept until he started taking up all the room in the bed at nine months old.

I was SOOOO tired and I didn't want to give up on the breast-feeding, so I just needed quiet really, which is hard to achieve when all your lovely mates want to come round and have a cuddle. When I left hospital I was in a kind of bubble. I suppose I didn't think about the fact that I would have to go home and get going straight away, having just been in labour for a day, with no chance to catch up on sleep. I didn't think about hitting the ground running and not getting over the labour exhaustion. In fact, those first few weeks I didn't ever catch up with myself on sleep or anything, and it became a cycle of feeding and sleepless nights as my poor old body tried to keep up.

I got home from hospital and the texts and messages started coming through thick and fast, but I didn't want to see everyone, if I'm honest. It's so overwhelming it's hard to explain, but you feel in a haze, like people can see in but you can't really see out. Actually, just keeping on top of the text messages was a job in itself. If you want to get in touch with a new mum, my advice would be to use voice note – it is a much more realistic way of getting an answer, mainly as it doesn't involve typing time! My milk was starting to come in – when your milk production gets going – and all I wanted was for us three to be tucked up in bed while I got to grips with the breastfeeding – it was something only I could do and I needed time to master it.

Despite the busy nature of our first few weeks, I will always remember the first night we brought the baby home and how we were just the three of us: we shut our front door and it was an amazing feeling knowing that this was my family forever now.

One of the first things me and Paul agreed on was that we were determined to do things our way, and that meant establishing our own routines and patterns. I suppose as mums, me and Billie have done things a bit differently – my mum moved in with Billie for two weeks after Nelly was born and the day she announced she had to go back to her own flat, Billie burst into tears! I was there every day too, every single day, helping Billie make bottles, getting Nelly to sleep and it was all so fresh for me when baby Paul arrived. It was such a special bonding time for me and Billie as sisters, but also for me as Nelly's Aunty Sam – I think I have seen her pretty much every day of her life. Billie is just as involved with baby Paul. In fact, in the first few weeks after he was born we all gave Billie a new name: the Baby Hogger! No one else could get a look in when she was around as she just loved cuddling him. We were all a bit worried about how Nelly would take to the fact that attention had shifted from her to baby Paul, but she was absolutely fine. You would get the odd little look now and again when me or Paul picked up the baby as if to say: 'With you two it's normally all about me, what's going on?' But she has always been affectionate with baby Paul and now he is older he is obsessed with watching her run around the place – he can't take his eyes off her and she is the perfect distraction for him if I need to get stuff done! She talks to him like a little mummy. I often hear her saying things like, 'What's the matter baby Paul, why you crying?' It is super cute and I feel lucky that they have been around each other so much – it will certainly make things easier for Billie when she has the next baby!

I have already said to Paul that with the next baby I would have immediate family only and then give myself two weeks before I had any other visitors, even close friends. That's my top tip: take the time you need to get to grips with it all and don't be embarrassed to be honest with people if you aren't ready for the hordes of well-wishers; real friends will understand.

Everyone wants to hear your birth story and, in my case, I also did an exclusive at home with *OK!* including a photo shoot, just to add on the pressure! I gave myself two weeks before I let the crew in – it was no way enough time, though I wasn't quite as bad as Billie, who did hers when Nelly was less than a week old! I know people can never understand the rush with these shoots straight after the birth, but, if you are in the public eye and you appeal to their readers, magazines will keep presenting attractive offers until they are too good to turn down. In our case, we saw it as money for baby Paul's education when he's older – the money is his to be put straight into a savings account – and so we went for it.

It is also genuinely a nice way to give the fans a look into your home and let them see the baby. I feel really lucky with my fan base. They are so loyal to me and have supported me through the ups and downs over the years, and me leaving *The Only Way is Essex*. Once I got pregnant I know that some mums also started following me on Instagram and I believe you should engage with the people who support you – I know I wouldn't be anywhere without my fans.

Of course, being offered a big shoot like that is an amazing opportunity and I would never knock it, but me and Billie were talking about it the other day and she said it was way too much too soon and she would definitely wait a bit longer next time. It is so hard because, just when you feel at your worst, you have to smile, give the ins and outs of your labour story, and put on heels and make-up when all you want to do is crawl into bed and sleep forever!

I did try and make it as easy on myself as possible – my friend did my hair and make-up, and I picked a photographer I knew well and who would put Paul at ease too (he hates shoots!). The *OK!* team were great and I asked them to only send the journalist writing the piece. I didn't want a huge entourage traipsing in and out of my house when it was our sanctuary – I hadn't even been outside myself yet! I didn't want to change baby Paul's outfit more than once: he just had a nice white babygrow on and we kept it as simple as these things can be.

I think looking back, the reason a 'reveal shoot' like that can be hard is because everything about your baby is an exclusive – that's what the magazine has bought and quite rightly they want all those details to be read for the first time in their magazine by their readers. It meant we couldn't release baby Paul's name or post any pictures of him on social media until the magazine came off the shelf. At a time when I wanted to shout out to the world that my beautiful baby was here, we had to keep him under wraps, and that is hard, which is why most people want to do the exclusive as quickly as possible and then get on with actually enjoying their baby. We did announce on social media the day after he was born and we used a picture of the three of us clasping fingers, which was a lovely shot. Billie also did some clever cropping of a picture of baby Paul on her shoulder where you couldn't see his face. It meant at least we could share something, especially after all the lovely messages we'd had on Twitter and Instagram.

Obviously on a shoot like this it's all about the glamour for their readers. They want to put you in all these outfits, they want to see your figure and if you've already lost the baby weight, and all you can think about is sore nipples, big breasts, often you're still bleeding and nothing feels remotely back to normal. The plus side is that we have beautiful pictures of the three of us so early on, which I wouldn't have taken if left to my own devices. You capture a lovely early moment that you can never recreate – those hazy, sleepy days. It also means that we have the interview, which is so raw, as you genuinely do forget the full details of the birth in many ways.

Tips for the early days

- Don't be afraid to put people off if you're too tired for visitors. Put yourself first because sleep is more important than EVERYTHING.
- If you're going round to see someone's new baby, make sure you're going to be useful, not to ask if the labour hurt and how many more babies the new mum wants!
- Make sure you bring food with extras for the freezer, and offer to take the ironing away, run the hoover round, wash up or go food shopping.
- If you're bringing dinner, come with paper plates and plastic knives and forks – a new mum has no time for dishes!

Bottle versus Breast – What Worked for Me

I exclusively breastfed baby Paul until I weaned him at six months, and even then he was still on breast milk and not formula. I am so proud that I went so far with feeding him myself and I can say that, until he was nine months old, he had never even had an expressed bottle. Even if I was on a job and left one in the fridge, it was like he decided to hold on until I came back, because when I got home he'd never needed the bottle. From the minute I found out I was pregnant I knew that breastfeeding was what I wanted and I was determined to make it work for us, however long it took and however difficult it was.

Breastfeeding is seen as one of the most natural things in the world for a mother and child to do. You have used your body to grow your baby, so it makes sense that you would use your body to feed and nurture your baby too, but I know it doesn't always work out for many women, for many reasons. I'm the last person to judge anyone for how they choose to feed their baby and, just because I have loved every minute and been lucky enough to be able to breast-feed so easily, I know that some women can't and some women just don't want to. Don't put any pressure on yourself: if you want to try then see how you get on. Whatever you decide has to work for you so that you can enjoy those first, early weeks. It is such precious time and it goes by so fast. I think it should be as stress-free as possible.

They are magical first weeks, but they are also about surviving too, so don't make it any harder for yourself than it already is. You worry so much in those early days about getting everything right, you don't need to feel bad about how you choose to feed and nourish your baby too – cut yourself some slack! I know I have posted some breastfeeding selfies and been quite open about how good I think it is, but that isn't from a position of judgement – I have truly just loved it and have wanted to celebrate my own choice. But that's what it is; what has worked well for us, not what I believe everyone should do (or feel bad about because they can't).

Like every other aspect of having a baby, every situation is different and we all do the best we can. Just as I don't think mums who bottle-feed their babies should be made to feel bad, I also feel the same about mums who breastfeed. I think if you are discreet then we shouldn't be made to feel like it is wrong to do it in public. Don't get me wrong, I'm not talking about getting your boob out in the middle of a meal for everyone to see and making a big deal of it; if you need a bit of privacy, I mean wearing easy-access clothes, having a shawl to hand if you need a bit of privacy, and just being able to feed your baby when you are out and about without stares. As you get to grips with it you will start to find it much easier. I'm amazed at the fact I can now unbutton in record time – sometimes with one hand!

I did worry about people looking at me in the beginning. Having been on TV, I was anxious that would make it harder to feed baby Paul when I was out and about with people staring at me, but it's actually fine and most other mums totally get it. Sometimes I just turn around if we're in a restaurant or a pub so that we're facing away from the table and the crowd. It doesn't have to be a big deal or make anyone feel uncomfortable. I haven't had any weirdness and so far it has been nothing but rewarding and amazing for me and I will be so sad when it stops.

There were many reasons why breastfeeding was so important to me, mainly because I knew how good it was for the baby. They get all the goodness of the food you eat and the antibodies in your milk protect them from early illness (eating so well made me feel great too). One of the main things I couldn't get over so early on was how convenient it was – I remembered all the faff of making up Nelly's bottles for Billie, how organised you had to be the night before and how fiddly the sterilising was. All the boiling water and exact measuring out of milk powder and making sure you have everything ready in advance, even when you might just want to rush out last minute – it wouldn't have been right for me. When you're feeding the baby yourself all you need when you leave the house are nappies and a muslin – it is so fuss-free with zero planning needed.

Make no mistake – the first two breastfeeding weeks are so hard. In the last weeks of pregnancy and immediately after the birth (but before your milk comes in), your body produces colostrum. It looks really weird and insignificant because it's clear, but it's the best thing you can ever give your baby. It's so good for your newborn and sometimes called 'high-octane' milk. It's full of antibodies, which not only protect your baby as they come into our world of bacteria and viruses, but also it's a bit like a laxative that helps them have their first poo, called meconium.

To produce great milk you need a lot of oxytocin (a hormone), which triggers the milk flow ready for your baby. It can be set off by hearing another baby cry or if you are feeling extra emotional. It can happen at any time and be massively inconvenient. There have been so many times I have looked down and seen wet patches where I had leaked – it isn't the best look! You need to be as relaxed and rested as possible to get the best milk supply, which sounds like mission impossible during the early days of motherhood!

My first challenge was to get baby Paul latched on. The midwife taught me how to do that in hospital in the first 24 hours and so we began our feeding journey. There's no point dressing this up: it was really hard at first. When they latch on it's like no other sensation in the world, the nipple goes up and under the roof of their mouth and the feeling is so weird. Your nipple is so soft and nice, and when they are really tiny they just want to be on you all the time. For those first few weeks, baby Paul definitely used my nipple as a dummy! You soon get to work out what positions result in the best feeds and it isn't always the more well-known 'cradle' position that feels the most comfortable. Early on I soon realised this didn't work for us and so started to hold him like a rugby ball under my arm because that's how I felt comfy and most natural – it might not be the way people expect breastfeeding to be done but that's what worked for me. As he got older it worked better when we would both lie down. We were really comfortable like that and it became our preferred way to feed, particularly if he was feeding in order to go to sleep – it definitely became his favourite night-time position after his bath and before bed. Once he was over six months, sometimes he would sit on my lap, facing me with his legs dangling down either side of mine and feed that way – this one worked well particularly if we were out and about.

After the colostrum comes the actual milk and, at the start, your body hasn't worked out how much milk it needs so it just all floods in. I remember one morning being in the shower and washing myself when all this milk started squirting out – it went absolutely everywhere! It does settle down though and that 'full' feeling does even out so your boobs don't feel so heavy all the time, just when you need to feed. It always amazed me that your boobs can get into a routine just like your baby. If by any chance baby Paul went over a feed and slept through, my boobs would immediately let me know it was feeding time even if the baby didn't! There is nothing like that feeling of a boob ready for a feed – it is the weirdest feeling ever – and the release when the baby has emptied it is the best feeling in the world!

Your milk comes in about four days after birth. Many mums, however, stop breastfeeding two weeks in. All the advice and blogs that I read up on for feeding tips said the same thing – that the first few weeks are the worst because it feels like the baby is on your boob the whole time, which is true, but once that proper milk comes in and you get your baby into a rhythm, it really does settle down. In those early days, sometimes I would be feeding literally all day long – some days I didn't move from the sofa apart from to go to the toilet. I used to say to myself, 'How am I ever going to get anything done?'

There were days that having a shower and washing my hair even felt too ambitious – baby Paul used me to feed, soothe himself, sleep and settle. When they are that tiny they just want to be on your chest all the time, warm and safe. It is lovely but it can also be overwhelming. But like every phase, this passes and everything evens itself out. My lifesaver was the V-shaped cushion that I used to support me holding baby Paul; whatever the position I was in, it took the pressure off my back and meant I could get comfy on the sofa or in bed. My top tip here is: if you are having one of those days with the baby glued to you, make sure you have your supplies to hand – lots of water, your phone or book, the TV remote and some snacks to keep your energy up. But also remember, this isn't what breastfeeding is like forever (being chained to the sofa and stuck inside), I promise you. It does get better and less intense and, once you're out and about, it's really convenient.

At the start he fed quite regularly through the night – 11.30pm-ish, 3am-ish and 6am-ish, and he was sleeping a lot. He fed more in the day, and that was harder in a way as it meant it was trickier to get out – I did find those constant feeding days hard and emotional. But we totally found our rhythm and it has been the best experience of my life. At six months baby Paul went from boob to cup so he could have his water but he also had a bottle with water in too when we were out and about. I was adamant about only introducing the bottle once he was well established at breastfeeding and I felt confident he was properly attached to the boob. I remember panicking about the idea of him having a bottle at six months, even if it wasn't for milk. I was really worried he would forget how to breastfeed and immediately prefer a teat. But I spoke to my health visitor and she reassured me that once the breastfeeding is established, they can't forget it – a bit like riding a bike I suppose!

I was so glad that I didn't need to use one of those nipple shields as I didn't want him to have to suck hard plastic – perhaps it doesn't sound logical to others but, in my mind, if I was going to use those then I might as well have given him a bottle; I just wanted everything to be as natural and gentle as possible. I was lucky that my nipples didn't get chapped or crack and I didn't need any cream. If you do suffer sore nipples that there are two schools of thought: the first is that you apply as much cream as possible before they start to bleed and scab over. The second is that it's better not to apply nipple cream at all and just let as much air as possible get to the nipples between feeds – i.e. sit with your boobs out when the baby isn't feeding! Damaged nipples can mean that the baby isn't latched on properly, so it might be worth seeking help for latching on. With all my babies I want to feed for at least six months and I can only hope that I find it as simple and rewarding each time round.

I only know how it is for us and, touch wood, baby Paul has had a really healthy first nine months and I believe a lot of that is due to his diet and being breastfed. I think it has helped him to not get anything more serious than a few colds and generally kept him fit and well. The World Health Organisation (WHO) recommends that babies should be exclusively breastfed until six months old, then breastfed with other foods till two years and beyond. I'm so pleased that breastfeeding worked for us, as I know not everyone is so lucky. I feel blessed that I got to give him the best start I could and that we both found the whole experience so enjoyable and rewarding. At the time I was writing this book, baby Paul still hadn't had formula and I was thinking about skipping it altogether and putting him straight on 'proper' milk of some description. For me the best thing has been that he loves breastfeeding as much as I do. It is our close and special time – which I appreciate all the more now that he is on the go and not so reliant on me during the day. Whatever is wrong, whether he's tired, teething or just a bit grumpy, a quick feed can solve just about anything and there is no better feeling for me as a mum than that.

Routine (Or Not, in Our Case)

Having a baby can come with so much pressure and one of the main reasons I wanted to do this book is simply to put down my experience and get the message out there that you should trust your instinct as a mum. When I first got pregnant, there were people telling me my life, as I knew it, was over. As soon as I had baby Paul people were quick to share their opinions with me on all the big stuff like breastfeeding. However, the main area where I got the most advice and horror stories was surrounding the issue of sleeping and routine.

I want to start by saying that in my experience (and I know that not everyone will share this viewpoint) I don't think newborn babies should be forced into a routine. I know that there are loads of mums out there who will massively disagree with this, and that's fine because what they do is up to them and I respect that 100 per cent, but strict early routines weren't for me. Paul agreed that we should get to know what our baby needed before we made any big decisions. I have known people immediately hire maternity nurses and push a baby into a rigid routine so early on – it's almost like the Victorian attitude of 'children should be seen and not heard'. The babies are brought home from hospital, swaddled, put in a separate room from their parents in the dark and left to cry it out. That just isn't something I feel okay about.

I approached sleeping like I tried to deal with everything else that came with new motherhood – I took my lead from baby Paul. As I have mentioned, we had lots of sleeping contraptions – we were so lucky that we bought, and were given, lots of different things to try. We had SnuzPods, Moses baskets and prams coming out of our ears, but Paul slept exclusively with us until he was nine months old. In fact, at the time of this going to print, I'm still trying to get him used to his cot and I'm not sure it's going to happen much before he turns one!

I firmly feel that from birth to around the age of four months they shouldn't be in a strict routine at all – I just don't believe they can cope with it or that they need it. All they need is you and to know that you are nearby; they need comforting and time to adjust to the outside world and you need to get to know them too. There is no better way to get to know your baby than to simply hold them, let them smell you and recognise your touch, allow them to hear your voice and have skin to skin as much as possible. In some cases they may have had a very traumatic birth to recover from – why would you want to put them in a basket and let them 'cry it out'? A baby doesn't even know what that means – they don't know they are being taught a lesson about settling themselves – all they know is that they want you. Admittedly, I know I was lucky that baby Paul didn't have reflux or colic or any of the other things that can make newborn babies cry for hours on end. But the truth is that babies cry, that's just what they do. But they don't normally cry excessively for no reason and I just always felt that it was my job to find out what baby Paul needed as quickly as possible so that he kept calm and knew I was there.

The thing I realised I had to come to terms with quickly was that no two days are the same with a new baby. Just when you think you have got it nailed, that they are moving on to one stage, they wake up and decide something completely different is on the cards. In those early days your baby is the boss of you – what they want is the priority and sometimes there is nothing you can do about a bad day other than get through it and start again the next morning. The problem with trying to force a routine is that if they don't play ball it leaves you feeling like a failure so early on in the parenting game and you end up putting even more pressure on yourself.

During those first few weeks, particularly if you are breast-feeding, the key is for everyone to sleep as much as the baby will let you. There is nothing more stressful than trying to feed a baby who hasn't had enough sleep, as they don't have the energy to latch on properly and then you worry about how much milk they are taking and get yourself all wound up. With that in mind, I was more than happy for Paul to sleep on me if that meant that he got his deepest sleep that way, because then he would eat more. In those early weeks I was a massive fan of whatever got us through the worst of it.

I think that babies let you know what they want and I didn't ever wake Paul up for a feed, as most of the time he seemed more than fine to let me know when he needed milk! I truly think that if you let them know that you are there and make them feel secure during those early months, then they will naturally fall into a rhythm that works for you both, because you will both be relaxed. By the way, I'm not saying it is easy – it isn't – but you have to be kind to yourself and not expect to have all the answers. It's like anything else that's new: you have to find your feet, get your confidence and learn on the job.

Obviously, sleep is a priority. The first few weeks are so hard and that is mainly because you are beyond tired in a way that it is impossible to comprehend. Even if you think you don't need a lot of sleep – watch out because you have no idea! For me, the priority was getting some rhythm to the day and I soon realised that, by the age of about six weeks, baby Paul naturally knew the difference between day and night. I feel that as long as you have that established, that's the main thing that will save your sanity in those early weeks.

Hands down, lack of sleep is the hardest thing but I took the attitude that, like all stages, it won't last forever. The baby's early months flash by so quickly, and I think that the obsession with when your baby starts to 'sleep through' means that you actually miss out on those precious times. Of course, the 3am feeds aren't ideal, but they will be over soon enough so you don't need to wish it away. Now he is older and always on the go, I actually miss those long feeds with Paul, where he would just doze on me all the time – maybe not at 3am, but you know what I mean!

Dummy versus thumb

We decided early on not to give baby Paul a dummy. It would have been the easiest thing to give him one right at the start, especially when he went through the phase of using my nipple for comfort and spending hours draped on my boob. There were people who told me that I was making life unnecessarily difficult for myself by not giving him a dummy and that I could take it away later when he was old enough to understand.

But I knew the suckling phase wouldn't last and that it would be harder to try and get him to give up the dummy when he was older, once he'd got attached to it. My theory is that relying on things like that means it's going to be painful at some point and if he was on the breast anyway, I figured I might as well do the tough bit at the start. I had my dummy until I was four, which is just embarrassing (and which my mum reminded me about when I was doing this book!). At the end of the day, he can't miss something he never had in the first place, so I stuck to my guns and put up with sore nipples instead.

Thinking back for this book I remember that Nelly had one at the start but she actually gave it up on her own. One day she just spat it out and so Billie didn't have all the drama of getting her to hand it over to Father Christmas in exchange for presents!

Routine and sleep

Sleep is an area where some people will have issue with what I'm saying, but all I can do in this book is tell you what worked for me and how I feel about the big stuff, and sleep is as big as it gets. It's like society has made it the only thing that defines good parenting: you are judged as a success or failure by how soon your baby sleeps through the night. But each mother and baby has different needs and thoughts on how to handle sleeping. You could go into any baby group and speak to a handful of mums about sleep issues and you will get a different answer from everyone. I also feel that this is where some mums feel pressured to give formula earlier than they might like to. If their baby isn't sleeping they are told it's because they are hungry and they should 'top them up' with a bottle. It's why people assume that the first food you should give when weaning is baby rice at tea time, because it will bulk them up and make them sleepy (it's also a reason I refused to do that with baby Paul, but more of that later). I wasn't obsessed with filling him up so that he slept, I just wanted him to eat things that made his gut healthy and that I knew were giving him all the goodness that he needed.

In the early days, I like to think that our house had a rhythm rather than a routine. In those first few weeks we had so many visitors and so many people would want to hold him, that any thought of routine (even if I had wanted one) would have been impossible. Baby Paul would often need a rub after a feed, which would actually take more time than the feeding, and in those early days either Paul or Gaynor would stay up with me and do the back rubbing so I could get some sleep once he'd had his milk. It was a way of making sure he got what he needed and that I managed to get rest, which affected things like my milk supply. We just went with the flow for those first six weeks. I was determined not to worry about it or put any pressure on myself to conform to what others thought I should do.

I would say, though, that if you do want to get into an early routine, try and limit your visitors. If people are popping round all the time (especially if they're unannounced) and you have just settled the baby, you will find that he or she is woken up all the time by being picked up and passed around. You could also try getting people to come at a certain time of the day when you know the baby is likely to be fussy and awake (or colicky). That way you get company and a break as someone else tries to settle him! This can work particularly well if your baby has wind and likes being held but you have mountains of washing to catch up on. An extra pair of hands is always invaluable, so make sure you work your visitors hard!

As the house was so busy, one thing I was glad about was that baby Paul didn't get used to silence during the day. If you don't have any other children, I can see how it is tempting to 'shush' people so the baby can sleep. In my view, if the days are busy and hectic and if you then keep the night-time quiet and cosy with candles and dimmed lights that make the place feel calm, they will quickly work out what is what. In the daytime I did put the dishwasher and hoover on – to be honest, when else do you get a chance to do the housework other than when they are sleeping? We were also in and out of the car a lot, which helped keep us active in the day and it also meant that baby Paul got used to sleeping in his car seat. In fact, all these months later, there is nothing that gets him straight off to sleep like being in the car – two minutes and he is out for the count.

I pretty much went back to work straight away, which I know isn't possible for many new mums. We had the *OK!* shoot two weeks after baby Paul was born, which obviously involved disruption and lots of people in and out of the house with cameras and lights. Two weeks after that I was on *Lorraine* when he was four weeks old to promote the show *The Baby Diaries*. That was daunting in every sense but mainly because I felt very on show. Every new mum will identify with the fact that there can be days where you feel all fingers and thumbs, particularly if the baby is having a bad or fussy day. It was enough that I actually had to get us both ready and out of the house (which, four weeks in, felt like mission impossible), but then I had to look camera ready as there were loads of paps there to capture every moment. I got out of the car at the studio and had to get baby Paul out of his car seat, put up the pram and settle him, all the time trying to look like a pro who had been doing it for years! The truth was that I had barely been out of the house myself and was still getting to grips with needing about nine hands to manage the whole 'being out' process.

I remember getting up at the crack of dawn to get from Essex to London (it was one of those hilarious mornings where, because I had somewhere to be, baby Paul decided to sleep in – isn't it so typical when they do that?), I had to get my hair and make-up done, and get the baby sorted and in the car so that we arrived at the ITV studio with enough time for me to feed baby Paul before going on air. It was the first time I had done it all with a baby and you rely so much on them playing ball with you but anything can go wrong in those early days – sometimes they just want you and that's that, everything else has to be ignored. Luckily it all went okay and I managed to do my promotion despite having no sleep and not feeling my best.

I am under no illusions: I know I'm lucky that I get to do my job and be totally there for my baby – I've been so selective about what I've done in baby Paul's first year, as my priority has been being a full-time mummy to him. It has influenced who I have worked with and I have naturally drifted towards brands and jobs that are baby-orientated and that I can easily make part of my everyday life, like me and Billie collaborating with My 1st Years. It all makes sense and it also means that they don't have a problem with me turning up with baby Paul in tow.

I suppose we just got into the work rhythm from day one; I have always worked and he has always come with me. Obviously, the main reason for this is because I was exclusively breastfeeding and I always had to be nearby, and the other is that I just wanted him close. My mum or Gaynor would come with me to look after him and take him off for a walk when I was in a meeting, but I wasn't leaving him behind. I know I'm really lucky and that perhaps it might become trickier as he becomes older, but for now it works perfectly for us. I'm not sure how easy it will be once he starts walking and getting into everything, but maybe by then I will feel more comfortable leaving him at home to come into town. We've had a few dummy runs where I've left Paul in charge for the day and it all went really smoothly, thankfully – or else it would have been the first and last time if it hadn't worked out! I did my mum thing of packing him his lunch and snacks in a little lunchbox, with a list of what needed to happen when. We got in the car together and drove to London, I went off to my meetings and the two Pauls went off to Harrods! They had lunch, ate my packed snacks of yoghurt and water (and milk, which he didn't drink!) that I had sent him off with, bought winter hats, and then came to meet me and we all had dinner. I felt that we had crossed the first and hardest hurdle. I thought baby Paul might be a bit funny about going for so long without a feed, but Paul said he didn't cry once and just ate all his food and played with no worries. As soon as I got back to him he made it clear he wanted me and was pleased to see, me but I don't think he actually missed me that much!

He is at the age where he is crawling everywhere, so now lunch meetings are harder as he doesn't want to be stuck in his highchair or buggy, he wants to be down on the floor with his toys, standing up and cruising around. He still loves a photo shoot, mainly as there is normally enough space in a studio for him to get about and amuse himself. He loves the music and the hustle and bustle of a shoot, plus there are always loads of people to fuss over him and play with him. I do think that being around so many different people since the very beginning has made him super sociable and really easy-going

– he will have a cuddle with anyone, loves company and can play happily pretty much anywhere.

I think because of that first TV show coming out just after he was born and me having so many PR commitments, I was forced to make it work. I was on the road, in and out of cars with him in and out of his pram, in bright TV studios and on press days. I look back now and I'm not sure how we managed! What I do know is that if I had been trying to get him into a strict routine at the same time as fulfilling all my work obligations, I would have driven myself completely mad. The only thing I could do was go with the flow.

I don't have a regular nine-to-five office-based job and my life isn't the same every day, which means that baby Paul's isn't either. He always comes before work and if he needs me at home, then I make that happen, but most of the time wherever I am he comes too. For the second ITV show we have done a lot of filming abroad as I had a few photo shoots in Spain and Portugal. We have had some breaks over the summer too, all of which has meant plane journeys, time differences and different villas and beds. Routine has been the last thing on my mind. If I am honest it can be challenging, because sometimes it's impossible for baby Paul to have a proper afternoon nap if he's in the car or buggy, but as a result he's very flexible about how he sleeps in the day, which means he isn't upset by change or being out and about. With some milk and a rock or push in his buggy, he's out like a light, whether he's at home or in a studio!

What I love most of all about what I do is that our family business, Minnies, is at the heart of my working week. I am so proud of all that we have achieved as a family, both with the shop and the online side. Me and Billie try and stay as involved as we can with the day-to-day running of things, but it's my mum and Aunty Libby who work full-time in the office and run it all so brilliantly. I try and pop in most days and go through paperwork, book appointments to discuss new online ideas, new seasonal campaigns and to talk about which bits are selling well and what looks we will both feature on our social media.

Often I go in with baby Paul under one arm and his baby walker under the other and set him down to cause carnage among the piles of paperwork and filing. He loves it there – there's loads of space for him to zoom around and he gets lots of attention and cuddles too. Being a family business means that it's totally informal and I will often get there to find Nelly running around too, which baby Paul loves. It's so nice that I can go to work and know that Paul is surrounded by family and people that he is excited to see, plus the shop is just down the road from home so it's all very local.

While I have never been too fussed by the daytime rules, I did try and introduce a bedtime routine once Paul hit six months. As he was that little bit older I knew he could handle it, plus he had already drifted into his own pattern, so really I was just reinforcing what he was already doing. Because Paul had been at work all day, it was important to make sure that the bedtime routine involved father-and-son time (not least as it gave me a break!). Once Paul came in at night, he would have a mad half-an-hour playtime with baby Paul, with lots of wrestling and tickling and cuddling – 'boy time' – before we started to calm things down to let baby Paul know that we were winding down for bedtime. I know thoughts on co-sleeping are divided but what follows is just what worked for us and not me telling you what to do. There are websites (with recommended guidelines) that can be found at the back of this book for more information.

Once playtime was over we ran a bath and that was Paul and baby Paul's special time – they usually bathe together and love splashing around. Baby Paul loved the water from the minute he was born and he adores bath time. Once he was all bathed and clean I would give him a little massage and put his pyjamas on, then we would lie on the bed and have milk. He would normally fall asleep on the boob and, once he was finished, I would tuck him up in our bed, safely surrounded by pillows so he didn't fall out. That went on until he was about eight months old and we decided that he was too big to share our bed. We came to this conclusion mainly as he was sleeping like a starfish and taking up all the room so that we had a corner of space while he had the whole bed! Once we did get into bed, he would kick and wriggle all night long. It got to the point where enough was enough so I started to give him his feed and then put him in his cot for the first part of the night, asleep, so that he could get used to it.

I know that co-sleeping attracts a lot of different opinion and that some people don't like it. I also know that the experts say that the best place for a baby to sleep under the age of six months is on his back in a cot or a Moses basket. I didn't deliberately decide to do something that's not recommended; we fell into a pattern of all sharing the bed early on when I was breastfeeding on demand, and sometimes the feeding lasted all night long in those early days. It was just easier to bring him into the bed and latch him on to settle him and it actually meant less disturbance for everyone at 3am as I wasn't getting in and out of bed, switching lights on and off, waking Paul but also stimulating the baby so he didn't go back to sleep. For me one of the great things was that he never fully woke up during those night feeds and I could just lay him down once he was finished and, as he was next to me, he would settle immediately and I could go straight back myself.

Don't get me wrong, I know that this isn't right for everyone at all and that I might get some stick for this, but I just did what felt right for us. I have found co-sleeping to be a really important and magical part of baby Paul's first year. Despite the fact that it worked safely for me, I have put some tips below for how you can enjoy it and make sure it is a safe and rewarding experience for you all.

Co-sleeping tips:

- Co-sleeping worked really well for me and my family, but there are risks involved when co-sleeping, and it's best to be informed. More information can be found at the back of the book.
- Don't fall asleep on the sofa with your baby – there is a danger they might fall off your chest and down in between the sofa arm and the cushions, leading to suffocation.
- Your mattress should be good and firm, as a saggy one could increase the risk of your baby suffocating.

- If you have a headboard and a frame, make sure that the mattress fits properly so the baby cannot slip down between the two and hurt himself.

- Use sheets and blankets and avoid covering the baby too much as this might cause overheating. If you have a duvet on the bed, make sure you pull it right down the bed, so it comes up no higher than your waist and doesn't gather around the baby's head.

- Make sure that your baby is warm but not hot. We also used a humidifier in our room for the first few months and that helped with airflow.

- When he is in the bed with you, keep your baby at the same level as your boobs, as it is easier for breastfeeding.

At the point of writing this book, baby Paul hadn't quite got used to sleeping in his own bed and made it clear that he wasn't impressed to be waking up alone in his cot and not in our bed where he enjoyed being! He screamed, but I wasn't keen on letting him cry it out and so we just kept trying. Paul suggested putting him in his own room but it felt like too much of a big leap (for me, anyway!) to go from our bed straight to his own room. We tried putting his cot in our room, but that decision came at the same time as his top teeth coming through (see the chapter on teething on page 241) and so all my brilliant plans went out the window as he reverted to wanting to be on the boob all the time in a way he hadn't been since he was tiny. We were on holiday when the big-time teething started and he was away from his familiar things, so it was just easier to put him back in the bed and try again once the teeth were through. He became clingy and only I would do, so he was back in with us.

I suppose I did worry that I left it too late to be stricter about sleeping in his own cot. It's probably my own fault for wanting him cosy next to me in those early months! At the point of doing this book, he hadn't mastered it and is back in with us, which perhaps isn't an example of me being very firm. I guess it shows that no one has the magic answers. We tried and, at this point in time, it isn't something I want to battle out with him. We will try again once he wants less breastfeeding and is feeling more settled, I'm just trying to go with the flow.

In a way, perhaps that's one downside of having such a hectic daytime routine; every day is different and we're rarely home for me to put him in his cot for naps every afternoon, which is a good way of getting them used to their cot or their own room. I decided not to stress about it though – that's just the reality of being a busy working mum. I can't always be at home for him to get used to things and he will make the leap when he is ready – he isn't going to sleep with us forever and before we know it, he will be a teenager sleeping all day long! Every baby and mum is different – that's the key thing to remember.

Getting Myself Back

There are no two ways about it: having a baby is the biggest thing that your body will ever do and there is no manual for how long the body and mind need to recover.

Something that makes me so annoyed about the society we live in is the pressure that is put on women, especially those in the public eye, to lose weight after they've had a baby. I want to say this upfront: I know that I'm lucky with my age and genes that my body settled down quickly after I had my baby, but I promise you that losing weight and 'getting my figure back' was the last thing on my mind after I had given birth. I haven't been in the gym six times a week and I haven't been living on a thousand calories a day. I assure you – there has been no magic weight wand!

The first month was a total haze of visitors, cards, presents, cake, tea, and hours and hours spent on the sofa with baby Paul attached to my boob – there were days when I felt I would never be myself again, when even the simplest of tasks, like loading the dishwasher, felt like climbing Mount Everest. The tiredness sometimes made me feel like I was walking through treacle and, when Paul went back to work, I couldn't wait for the moment when he walked back through the door so that I could talk to another grown-up. I was overwhelmed by love and the huge sense of responsibility I felt for protecting our tiny baby, and I also felt mega emotional about everything. I cried at everything and I didn't really want to leave the house unless I had to for a work thing. Going out on my own felt like a massive deal, and in the early days I wasn't quite ready for it. I have decided that I want all my babies in winter, as it is the perfect excuse for staying tucked up inside if you don't quite feel ready to face the world! It felt like a real milestone getting us up and ready and out – in the early weeks I managed dinner at my mum's, Billie's and Gaynor's, and that was as adventurous as it got!

I've talked a bit about the physical side of having a baby, and how for some it can be more traumatic than for others. It has been harder for the friends I know who have had a caesarean, as that has clear physical downsides and limits you to what you can do imme-diately afterwards, and you are obviously in more pain with the scar and everything. I'm so glad that I didn't have to get over the side effects of an epidural as well as the actual birth – I know it can take a few hours to be able to make sense of what has happened and to also feel your legs again.

That magic six-week mark you hear talked about – the time when you become more used to being a mum and having a little one to care for – was real in my case. When baby Paul was six weeks old I felt like myself again; it was like the sleep deprivation fog had lifted and I felt alive again. I don't know what happened between weeks four and six, but during those two weeks it was like I flowed back into my own body. I felt physically and mentally like myself. For me it was massively helped by the breastfeeding as I could actually feel my uterus contracting and could see the benefits breastfeeding had for me as well as knowing baby Paul was getting the best start. It was like every time he latched on I got a mini work out! I was unprepared for how much I could feel everything being pulled back into place in my stomach: the body is such an amazing thing. The first time you get those sensations it can be shocking as it does hurt a bit, but don't worry, there's nothing wrong.

The weird thing is that, since I've had baby Paul, my metabolism has completely changed and I can eat whatever I want for the first time in my life (it's the same for Billie too – she's at her slimmest since having Nelly). All in all, I put on about two stone during my pregnancy but it didn't worry me – though by the end I felt so heavy with the water retention that I probably looked like a Christmas pudding! It was hard at times, especially given that just before I found out I was expecting baby Paul, I felt like I was in the best shape of my life. For about a year before I fell pregnant I had worked hard at my body. I wasn't ever really a naturally skinny girl so I always watched what I ate, and when I got the exercise bug my whole figure completely changed.

Before the baby, I can still remember what it was that kick-started me deciding to lose weight and make the much-needed change: a set of really terrible and unflattering bikini shots in the paper. I just woke up one day and decided that was that – I was sick of seeing myself looking pasty and bloated in photos taken from unflattering angles. Once I started working out, suddenly I had a small waist and brilliant abs and a good bum, it was a world away from my look on *TOWIE*, where I had such an unhealthy diet fuelled by booze and then bad food choices when I had a hangover. I was never really overweight but I was mega bloated and uncomfortable – I suppose at my heaviest I was ten stone. Don't get me wrong, I didn't spend my time falling out of clubs and eating kebabs, but I knew I had to take myself in hand. Everyone has a tipping point and I found mine.

Was I obsessed? Probably a little bit. I defy any girl not to suddenly discover they love fitness and become a little bit fixated on it. For me, I found that once you start putting in all that hard, physical work, you then don't want to eat crap. It becomes easy to cut down on your food because once you start to see results then you don't want all that hard work to be wasted, so you do get stricter and sometimes it can take over a little bit. But that is another bonus of having a baby – any thoughts about yourself go right out of the window. There is barely time to go for a wee, let alone look at yourself in the mirror wondering if you've lost a few pounds!

Talking of going to the toilet, I weed for England as soon as I had the baby. Literally I couldn't stop and all this liquid kept on coming out. Within a week I probably lost seven pounds – I lost all that excess fluid and all the bloating in my legs and face went down. It helped that baby Paul came two weeks early so I didn't gain even more that extra fluid and weight. Poor Billie was ten days late with

Nelly and she was so uncomfortable she couldn't wait to give birth. I never felt at the end of my tether and I didn't gain that last bit of 'overdue weight' that is often the hardest to shift.

It wasn't until baby Paul was six weeks old that I started to see a change in my body. By that time I hadn't really gone out much or got dressed (apart from the odd magazine shoot and TV appearance!), I was just tucked up at home trying to get to grips with breastfeeding and taking in all the huge changes that had come our way. I was sat on the sofa in my house all day every day, just going to the toilet or breastfeeding! I always say that one of the great things about having a winter baby is that being bikini ready was the last thing on my mind in January. I spent all my time wrapped up in layers and it genuinely wasn't a worry of mine.

Paul was such a hungry baby that the more he fed the more calories I burned. I could feel those muscles coming back together and, for the first time in my life, I felt starving hungry all the time. Luckily we had both of our mums on hand to bring round delicious dinners – they are both great cooks and that was the best thing that anyone could have done for us at that time. We had all sorts and none of it was low fat or diet food. We're talking spaghetti bolognese, big roast dinners with all the trimmings, ham, egg and chips – pretty much anything that was delicious and would give us energy. When people brought round food they often made extra so that we could have it for lunch the next day or freeze some.

What I would say is that being in the public eye didn't automatically (or miraculously) mean that my baby tummy immediately disappeared – far from it! The truth is that I never thought it would get back to normal again. Just after I had baby Paul I remember going to the toilet and pulling down my tracksuit bottoms to have a look at my tummy and the damage that had been done. The best way I can describe my stomach area is that it resembled a jelly-like mess. Actually, it was like mush. As the days and weeks went on it did tighten up and as all the water went, so my face and feet went back to normal. Luckily for me, I had seen it all before with Billie and also witnessed that she then got back into the best shape of her life, so I tried not to think about it too much. (Though I did hope I had also inherited my mum's brilliant genes, as she bounced straight back after both of us!) The tummy thing had been a running joke between Billie and me after she had Nelly, so when she came to see me in hospital the day after I'd had baby Paul, she was like, 'So Sam, how's your tummy?'

Before I got pregnant I weighed 8st 12lbs and when baby Paul was a month old I weighed in at 10st 3lbs.

Even six months after baby Paul was born I still didn't have my six-pack and I certainly wasn't a perfect size 8 – the truth is that I didn't feel pressured to be either. Every mum understands more than anything that running a house, having a baby, going back to work, weaning and breastfeeding means that it's impossible to put your figure first. There is a bigger job to be done: dealing with all the chaos and wonder that comes with looking after your brand-new baby. It isn't just the washing, feeding and burping – you can wake up with your day all planned and something suddenly derails it. The other day baby Paul pooed all over the sofa, which meant I had to strip off all the covers, put them through the washing machine, dry and flatten them out before attempting to wrestle them all back on. That literally took the whole day!

When baby Paul was eight weeks old I started a fitness shape-up with *Closer* magazine and they offered me a personal trainer at home whenever I wanted. It was exactly as you would imagine with lots of embarrassing 'before' shots of me in shorts and crop tops, but it was also a good incentive. It wasn't just giving my body an overhaul but it was also good for my mind too. Initially the trainer came three times a week and I couldn't believe how wobbly and flabby my so-called core felt! Your core also includes your lower back muscles and your newly out of line pelvic and hip bones. It sounds silly, but I think it was then I really understood that my abs were in need of a serious reboot – they had suffered a major trauma! I also read that lack of core strength is why your back starts to hurt when you carry around your baby – because your stomach muscles are giving zero support, your back has to work twice as hard to keep you strong and standing tall.

The straightforward truth is that, no matter how fit you were and how long you could hold a plank for, those first few sessions in those first few months are all about getting back to basics. Don't think about picking up where you left off – it will be hard work. You won't suddenly find your old strength after one mega session, you will simply want to sleep forever!

The first thing the trainer did was to feel my tummy muscles in order to see if the muscles had fully separated or just thinned. Both scenarios are common during pregnancy, and some people suffer more than others. The trainer taught me that there is a simple way to check how much your muscles have been affected by pregnancy.

Lie on your back and make your abs go as hard as they can and press down into your abs above and below your navel. If you can feel any soft gap between the muscles then they have come apart. A gap of one to two finger widths is normal and, in time, should close on its own. If the gap is wider than that, you may need to get medical help to make sure that it closes properly.

Once the trainer was happy that my abs were okay and strong enough for me to start exercising, we started doing the usual home work out routine of squats and lunges with light weights. She also decided that, due to my previous fitness levels, we would do a little bit of cardio too. It's true that any incentive will get you going and stop you making excuses, and knowing that I had to wear a bikini for a magazine shoot was just about as good as it gets in terms of motivation! When I saw the magazine on sale I felt like I had worked hard and I was happy with the results.

I wasn't in the best shape of my life but I genuinely felt okay and I got a lot of really nice feedback from real mums out there who appreciated that I looked realistic and not airbrushed. I still had a jelly tummy and some weight to shift on my thighs but it was all going in the right direction and it felt good to have got started. I did the shoot and made myself a promise that I would keep up with the exercise, not least as it would be good 'me time'. But of course life with baby Paul took over again and I did what we all end up doing –

bursts of exercise but nothing that committed me to a rigid training programme. I had great intentions and threw myself into it but then, as all mums will know, it stops when life (and breastfeeding) takes over. It's impossible to commit to regular training slots every week in those first few months, mostly as you never know what the day will bring. Even by the time baby Paul was one, I hadn't really got into any kind of training regime. I just didn't have time and, because I had lost the weight, it wasn't a priority.

If you're still breastfeeding once your baby hits the six-month mark, then you can burn up to five hundred calories a day. I definitely lost more weight feeding baby Paul after he turned six months than I did at the start. And, for me, it has been far more help in shifting the final, stubborn baby pounds than any kind of diet has been. In fact, weirdly, when he hit the nine-month mark I went through a phase when the weight fell off me and that final half a stone just disappeared. I certainly didn't do anything differently or change my diet in any way to help me lose weight. I put it down to the teething as baby Paul did become clingier and was feeding throughout the day and twice in the night, so that might be the reason for the extra calories being burnt up.

Before you start to exercise, remember some key rules:

- Wait for your bleeding to stop – if your flow gets heavy again after initially stopping, it can be a sign that you're overdoing it, so take it easy and listen to your body

- Start back slowly, and if you have had a caesarean then make sure you don't do anything more strenuous before six weeks apart from going for walks with the pram. If you overdo things it can set you right back. Ask your GP about returning to exercise at your six-week post-natal check.

- The hormone relaxin is responsible for softening the ligaments and joints during pregnancy and childbirth. Sometimes this hormone can linger in the body for up to six months after you give birth and can lead to wobbly and unstable joints and maybe a loose pelvis. Just make sure you take it a step at a time and don't presume you will be back to where you left off – pregnancy obviously changes your figure but also your fitness levels.

- Make sure that once you start exercising again, you drink plenty of water (especially if you are breastfeeding). I take water everywhere with me whether I exercise or not, but if you're hitting the gym, make sure you take a big bottle to rehydrate you.

- Don't substitute exercise for rest. You still need to sleep when you can and when the baby does. Sleeping and healing your body needs to be your immediate priority – your baby needs a healthy mum more than he needs a skinny one!

Tummy Exercises for an Easy Shape Up

(after six weeks and a doctor's sign off)

Pelvic Bridge:

- Lie on your back with your feet hip-width apart and your knees bent.
- Breathe in as you pull in your abs, as if drawing them to your spine.
- Tilt your pelvis right up, making sure that your hips are off the floor and shaping yourself into a bridge.
- Lower down into the starting position.
- Repeat 5 to 10 times, building up from 2 to 5 reps.

Bicycle crunches

- Lie on the floor and stretch your legs out straight with your arms down by your sides and your lower back pressed to the ground.
- With your hands behind your head, contract your abdominal muscles as you lift your shoulder blades off the ground.
- Straighten your right leg at a 45-degree angle from the floor and turn your upper body to the left.
- Bring your right elbow to your left knee.
- Switch sides and alternate, like you are pedalling a bike.
- Do your crunches for 30 seconds, then rest, and repeat 4 times.

Plank

- Lie flat, facing the ground, with your forearms flat on the floor. Your elbows should be positioned under your shoulders.
- Place your legs together with your feet on the ground.
- Raise your body upward by straightening your body in a line.
- Hold this position with your abdominal muscles engaged for 30 seconds.
- Repeat 4 times.

Side plank

- Lie on your side with your elbow under your shoulder.
- Stack your hips and feet, stabilise your core and lift your hips off the floor until your body forms a straight line.
- Hold for at least 30 seconds.
- Repeat on the other side.
- You can add leg lifts to the side plank to improve stability and core strength.

Wall sit

- Lean against a wall while standing straight.
- Slide down until your knees form 90-degree angles. Hold this position while keeping your abs contracted for 30 seconds.
- Repeat 4 times.

Scissor kicks

- Lie flat on your back with your legs out in front of you.
- Engage your abdominal muscles by drawing in your belly button to your spine and raise your legs up so that they are 45 degrees to your hips.
- Once at 45 degrees, create a scissor-like movement with both legs at the same time – raising and lowering them, keeping your legs near the floor for maximum effort.
- Complete scissor kicks for 30 seconds, rest, and repeat 4 times.

Squat

- Place both your feet shoulder-width apart with your toes pointing slightly outwards.
- Looking straight ahead, bend your knees and at the hips making sure that your knees point towards the toes.
- Bend your knees until your thighs are parallel with the floor, making sure that your back remains between 45 and 90 degrees to your hips. You can use your arms to balance you.
- Push through your heels and return to a neutral standing position.
- Complete 4 sets for 30 seconds each.

Reverse lunges

- Stand upright and contract your abdominal muscles to stabilise your upper body.
- Lift your left foot off the floor and step backwards.
- Bend your right knee to form a 90 degree angle between your thigh and calf, while lowering your left knee toward the floor.
- Push yourself upward with your thigh muscles to return to the starting position.
- Repeat with the other leg for 30 seconds.
- Repeat 4 times.

Being in the Public Eye

It's funny really: as a new mum you spend so much time celebrating the small achievements like getting showered and dressed, getting all the washing done so that the laundry basket is empty (even if it's only for approximately eight minutes before the baby is sick over everything again), changing the bed sheets – basically getting through another day with everyone still in one piece. But sometimes it can feel like there are always people waiting to criticise you. Don't get me wrong, I don't mean other mums, or fans and supporters; it just felt in the first few months that sometimes I couldn't do right for doing wrong with some of the press and interaction on social media.

Looking back, you could argue that I opened myself up to it by going back out into the public world so early on, but I had commitments and doing the press for *The Baby Diaries* was my job – that's what I do. But just after you've had a baby and you're feeling vulnerable, it's easy to let it drag you down, especially with all those extra hormones swirling round.

My first taste of it was when we revealed baby Paul's name in our *OK!* interview – for some reason, picking a traditional name (after his dad) sent the media into meltdown. As I've said before, it's a Knightley custom and I think it's a lovely simple name. Baby Paul's middle name is Tony, after Paul's brother. It's the second name on his birth certificate, we don't use it every day, it's not a hyphenated name and yet the papers insist on calling him Paul Tony. I find it hard because that's not his name: his name is Paul Knightley; my name is Samantha Elizabeth Faiers, but no one calls me Samantha Elizabeth. I feel like whatever we had picked, people would always have an opinion. It's like when I was pregnant and people would ask if I had any names on my shortlist. I'd mention one and the person I was speaking to would say, 'Oh don't use that name. I had a friend called that at school and he was a right bully!' And so on.

Luckily we didn't find out the sex so we didn't get too drawn into those early name chats, but I soon learned it was better not to discuss it at all. People always have an opinion and some people really didn't like our choice, but that's fine, as they don't have to live with it or like it – we do. Whatever we had called baby Paul would have been wrong for some, and while they're entitled to have their view, being mean about a baby online is the pits as far as I'm concerned. It's weak and says more about the people doing it than anything else. Some of those comments on my social media were out of order – they were slagging off a baby who can't fight back and just because of his name! I think that was the first sign of my protective mummy mode coming out definitely!

I remember saying to Paul that I couldn't believe all the fuss and, if I'm honest, I didn't really understand why people cared that much over such a simple, inoffensive name. If we had called him something mental like Tree Knightly then I might have understood it!

But the whole name thing pales into insignificance when it comes to women in the public eye and baby weight – the press are so up and down in what they say and write, if you took it seriously you would go mad.

I mentioned earlier on the time just after the baby was born that I went on *Lorraine* to promote the first ITVBe show – I was exhausted, baby Paul was four weeks old and I had been up for two nights in a row breastfeeding non-stop. I was done in and my face was all swollen with tiredness and dehydration. It's easy to forget in those first few breastfeeding months that water is vital, and it soon affects you in terms of puffiness and dark circles under your eyes if you haven't had enough fluids. You can look lined and puffy through lack of water – never mind the lack of sleep!

So on the day I ventured out for the first time I had other concerns that felt more important than whether or not my face looked so puffy my eyes had almost disappeared. Admittedly I wasn't looking or feeling my best, but like most new mums, I hoped that the make-up would cover the worst of it. Apparently the papers couldn't make their minds up – one headline screamed out: 'New mum Sam Faiers shows off her incredible post-baby body in chic shirt and tapered trousers combo as she takes baby Paul for his first-ever chat show appearance.' Which, by the way, made me laugh out loud as, believe me, I wasn't 'sensationally slim' as they described me in that article – far from it. Nor was I was 'sporting a sun-kissed look' – it was February, I hadn't been in the sun since the previous October and I hadn't fake tanned. I just had lots of blusher on!

Of course there were the usual hundreds of comments underneath the story – lots of support, but also lots of women asking what my 'secret' was and what 'quick fix' I had subjected myself to. All this when in truth I was just doing all I could to survive and get to grips with it all. My figure wasn't the last thing on my list of priorities – it wasn't even on the list!

The very next day a magazine ran the following headline: 'What has Sam Faiers done to her face? Is this the result of fillers or is she just a tired new mum?'

So in the space of 24 hours I had gone from 'sunkissed' and 'flaunting' my 'amazing' body to a filler addict who was prepared to poison the breast milk I was producing and feeding to my brand new baby – all in the pursuit of a smooth face!.It was the classic, if you haven't got a story or a quote then just make it up.

I want to make it clear here that I know the score with my job and I have a thick skin. If I was going to be sensitive about every single thing written since I've been in the public eye, I would never leave the house! I know how it works and Paul definitely learned that with all the PR surrounding *The Baby Diaries*. No one can live your life but you, and whether it's a social media post or hours and hours of filming cut down to 90 minutes by producers wanting to make a great, headline-grabbing show, only you know what's real and what's not. I would never do anything to my body or face at the age of 25 – why would I? And I definitely wouldn't do anything to myself when

I was breastfeeding my baby and filling my body with goodness to pass on to him.

But the fact is that some people will look at those headlines and believe them, or at least believe there might be some truth in them and that I've used drastic diets or needles to help get my pre-baby body back. It annoys me because it isn't true and it puts unfair pressure on new mums, some of whom are too tired to do anything at all. It's irresponsible, not least as a lot of my followers are young, and now I have baby Paul I'm even more aware of how important it is to be a good role model. I don't want people thinking there is some magic trick I'm not sharing – it's just the way I'm built and the way it is for now. It doesn't mean it will always be like that or be as easy to get back in shape after every baby – I might not be so lucky next time!

It's also about keeping it real for all the other new mums out there, who might just assume that people like me hand our babies over to nannies and spend all day in the gym and having facials – which couldn't be further from the truth. When I 'm not working, my day is genuinely just like all the other mums I know – it's all feeding times, baby groups, shopping at Tesco and getting on top of the washing basket. There is no Essex glamour to my life most of the time and that is just the way I like it. It's called being a full-time mum and, for me, what's the point of having a baby if all you care about is getting your abs back or getting a fake tan every week?

Headlines like the one about me having fillers make me want to shout back, 'Give me a break, I'm knackered here! Sleepless nights or a facelift – which do you think it is given I had a baby four weeks ago?!'

I know I've said before but people do forget that I was so young when I was on *TOWIE*. When it began I was 19 and now at 25 I look very different, but so do all my mates. Everything changes during those years; your bone structure becomes different, I've lost weight, I've changed all my make-up and beauty regime – you just grow into your own skin the older you get and the healthier you live. I have no problem with people who have face work done and are open about it – each to their own – but I think it is dangerous and unfair for people to be told things about me that simply aren't true.

In the end, I just have to do what's right for me and mine, which is the same for every mum and dad out there. Some headlines might make me laugh, and some make me cringe, but at the end of the day what matters most to me are my fans, my friends, my family, and of course the lovely little unit I've created with my two boys.

Family Food
for Breastfeeding,
Weaning
and Beyond

There is no doubt that a huge part of why I have shifted the weight and feel so good is down to my healthy diet. It has become a huge part of how I live my life and make sure we all stay fit and healthy. It wasn't so much about getting back in my pre-baby jeans (although that was a nice bonus for me when it eventually happened, it wasn't my motivation), it was about feeling my best.

It's obviously been well documented that I've been dealing with Crohn's, but when it came to the pregnancy (and ever since) I've never felt better. Some other Crohn's sufferers I've spoken to say the same thing – that pregnancy really keeps the symptoms at bay – but of course it all depends on the individual. Once I had baby Paul I was determined to keep things as natural as possible now that I was off my drugs and trying to control things with a pure and healthy diet that would help me get through those exhausting first few months.

When I met Paul, I had my flare-ups almost sorted and, on the advice of my doctors, had been taking my medication. At that point I was down to just taking azathioprine (an immunosuppressant) daily to keep everything at bay. Paul is so into his healthy eating knowledge and had actually spent loads of time learning all about different food combinations after his brother Tony fell ill. In order to help his brother, Paul decided that he wanted to find out more about the role that food and diet could play in helping Tony get back on his feet. When we met I told him about my condition and my wish to find a non-medical way to keep everything in remission. It was then he suggested looking into how diet could help keep my triggers in check. In a way it was obvious as Crohn's is inflammation of the bowel, so why not see if eating an anti-inflammatory diet could help the symptoms?

This also came at the same time as me wondering about the drugs I was taking and what the long-term side effects were. I want to be clear here: I'm not suggesting that I was misled by my doctors or that people with Crohn's who take the drugs I did, and medication like it, should stop. I'm also not saying that the drugs prescribed for Crohn's are bad for you. Like everything else in this book, this is about my own personal choice and my wish to educate myself on how food and the right diet could help keep me in remission once I was discharged from my doctor and had everything under control.

I struggled massively with the thought of being on drugs for the rest of my life and I wanted to see if there was another way. I know there are people who will disagree with my choice, and I totally respect that, but it was just for my own peace of mind that I wanted to explore other things. I did worry about the potential side effects of being on medication forever. At the start, I was so very ill that I just took what I was given in order to guarantee that the symptoms didn't come back – that was my only priority. But as things settled down again and I was discharged from my doctor, I began to weigh everything up.

Food and Crohn's

It was around this time that Paul's research led to a naturopath named Dr Wallach, who is trained in human health, but also in animal health as well. His theories are based on the results of an agricultural industry that eliminated 900 diseases in animals that still plague humans. He doubled animal lifespans and he's on a mission to do the same with humans. He isn't a medical doctor – he has a doctorate in veterinary science and a doctorate in naturopathic medicine – but he does have 35 years of experience in nutrition. He argues that to be healthier all we have to do is absorb the right nutrients for a long enough time – he believes that the body has an in-built ability to heal itself if it has access to all the right things.

Dr Wallach believes that the food-related treatment of Crohn's includes a high-fibre diet, and taking folic acid, vitamins A and B12, calcium and magnesium, zinc and chromium. I largely follow an anti-inflammatory diet and some of the key herbs include: turmeric, aloe vera, ginger, cinnamon, boswellia, camomile and neem.

The 12 anti-inflammatory ingredients include beetroot, blueberries, broccoli, flaxseed oil, garlic, ginger, olive oil, onions, seaweed and spinach.

When my Crohn's symptoms first came on, I was treated as soon as I came out of the *Big Brother* house and, when I had the initial flare-up, I was on steroids, the shake diet (which you are put on as soon as you are diagnosed with Crohn's), azathioprine and antibiotics. I recovered from that episode very quickly and then started reintroducing food to see if it was possible to identify any clear triggers so that I knew what to avoid and what would set me off. I was going back to my doctor every three months and getting another prescription for the drugs I'd been given without me asking any questions about other ways of managing things. It suddenly dawned on me that I would be taking them for life, so I was worried about what these drugs would do to me and my organs over the decades, especially as I'd started using them in my early twenties.

Once I was back on an even keel, I decided to look into some of the side effects of what I was taking and they included: migraines, swollen joints, vomiting, bleeding gums, chest pain and back or side pain.

When I started researching it, I was feeling fit and healthy and eating pretty much what I wanted. When I was diagnosed, the doctors had warned me against acidic foods, but I was eating them and feeling okay. The advice at the beginning had been to keep my food neutral (i.e. white-coloured food) but there was also some advice out there that stated this was the worst sort of food you could eat with Crohn's. The truth about the disease is that, at this point in time, the medical establishment doesn't know where it comes from, its cause or how to cure it, so all those who suffer from it can only do their best to live with it the best way they can. I chose to throw away my pills and try and control it through diet and lifestyle. So far, it's working well for me. I focused my attention on eating an anti-inflammatory diet, as well as taking various vitamins and supplements, in particular: Youngevity's 'Mighty 90' – I take four tablets a day and in just one there is more goodness than you could eat in your diet in a week. Some of the 60 minerals present in each tablet include: calcium, magnesium, phosphorous, potassium, sodium, chloride, copper, zinc, and iron. Each pill also contains omega-3, omega-6 and omega-9, as well as 16 vitamins and 12 amino acids.

I also drink Kefir, which is fermented milk and is a brilliant source of nutrients. It's normally made using cow's or goat's milk and by adding kefir grains to the milk – these grains are cultures of yeast and lactic acid bacteria. Over 24 hours the microorganisms in the grains multiply and ferment the sugars in the milk and turn it into a kefir drink. The grains are strained out of the liquid and, if you want, they can be re-used.

The microorganisms in kefir are also called probiotics and they help with digestion, weight and mental health. Yoghurt is known as the best probiotic food, but kefir is a much more concentrated version – it has about 30 strains of bacteria and yeasts. It also has certain probiotics that protect against infections.

Kefir can help protect against things like osteoporosis, as it's a great source of calcium. It contains high levels of vitamin B12, calcium, magnesium, vitamin K2, biotin, folic acid, enzymes and probiotics. Most importantly for me, it's thought to restore the balance of the gut and help with friendly bacteria. There is lots of evidence that probiotic foods can help with all sorts of digestive problems such as IBS, ulcers and Crohn's. It's also great for anyone who is lactose intolerant.

My feeling is that these supplements can't be doing anything wrong to me and, with all the various plus sides, they are taking care of all the important aspects of my health, and my gut health in particular. Obviously I know that a few vitamins haven't 'cured' me, but it's a lifestyle I'm committed to and I've also had loads of messages from women with Crohn's who say that their symptoms were kept at bay by pregnancy and a change in diet. I came off my pills before I got pregnant but who knows, perhaps the hormonal changes to my body have also helped to keep me in remission, alongside the new diet I'm following? All I know is that I feel good, strong, healthy and in the best place to feed baby Paul and keep him well and happy.

Did you know that over 50 per cent of your immune system is taken care of by your digestive system? Basically, lots of 'good' bacteria will kill the bad stuff and that's what keeps you fit and well.

I believe in living as healthy a life as possible and I try and stay away from painkillers and antibiotics as much as I can. I want to make clear this is just my opinion and I am not for one minute telling you not to go to the doctor if you are ill. Obviously I'm talking about avoiding medication for everyday stuff like colds and headaches, not anything serious. For me, the thought of taking anti-biotics means that it would disturb all the good bacteria I work so hard to keep balanced with diet and lifestyle. I believe that if you unsettle this then it leads to digestive issues and problems with your immune system. Basically, if you can't take in all the nutrients that you need because the balance in your gut isn't right, then your body won't have the fuel to keep you energised and well.

I really want to make it clear again that I'm simply being honest about what worked for me and what I believe. I'm not saying that I'm medically qualified or some kind of doctor, I know I'm not, but we all live the best way we know how, don't we? And this is how I do things.

The no-medication-unless-you-really-need-it attitude extends to baby Paul too. I know that there will be times when I will need to take him to the doctor, and that is not what I'm talking about. I'm talking about the day-to-day stuff that I try and manage myself. So far, I know we have been really lucky that he has only had a few colds and some teething trouble so I haven't needed to give him any medicine. Don't get me wrong, I know lots of people like to give their babies Calpol to help with temperatures and colds, but I prefer natural methods. When he is bunged up we swear by our air humidifier to moisten the air in our bedroom where he sleeps so that it isn't so dry and catching in his throat, making him cough and his chest worse. A few drops of Olbas oil on a tissue near the bed throughout the night also works really well when he's having trouble with congestion. The first time he wasn't well he was on my boob all day long and I made sure that I was packing myself with goodness and passing it on to him, which seemed to get him back to normal fairly quickly.

When baby Paul has had a few colds I've also used chest rubs that smell of eucalyptus to clear his nose and chest. If he's been blocked up and full of snot, then I've squirted some breast milk up both his nostrils, which is a bit of a messy operation but it definitely does the trick! As a last resort, you can buy one of those baby snot extractors that you put at the entrance of their nose and suck out all the snot with – it's pretty gross but also really effective when they are really bunged up.

The other thing I find really hard now he's a bit older is if he is eating with a cold and full of phlegm. Sometimes when he is chewing, the back of his throat gets blocked up and he does that thing where they gag, which terrifies me. I try and stay calm obviously, but it's pretty much the only thing that makes me a bit anxious.

Back to the food: I want to be clear that I'm not a mega strict 'clean eater'. As I have said, I eat more now than I ever have and I don't cut anything out to follow a 'diet', I just try and pick things that I know will help me keep on a healthy track.

I'm not saying that you have to go out and buy a whole new fridge full of food and eat nuts and seeds all day long, but there are foods that have definitely helped with my anti-inflammatory needs and I make sure these make their way on to my plate as much as possible:

- Green leafy vegetables are not only anti-inflammatory but they are also rich in antioxidants that help your cells repair them-selves. Swiss chard, for example, is very high in antioxidant vitamins A and C, as well as vitamin K, which protects the brain against stress.

- Bok choy is a brilliant source of antioxidant vitamins and minerals.
- Celery has lots of antioxidant and anti-inflammatory properties that help with blood pressure and cholesterol, as well as helping to prevent heart disease. It also helps to lower inflammation and is great at helping your body to fight off infection.
- Beetroot is full of folic acid, manganese, potassium and magnesium, as well as being packed full of anti-inflammatory goodness.
- Broccoli is packed with antioxidants and is great at soothing inflammation, and also recognised as generally having all-round goodness that helps the body to stay fit and well.
- Blueberries –these are full of quercetin (found in olive oil too) and are known for fighting inflammation. Some studies have shown that blueberries are also good for improving memory.
- Pineapple contains bromelain, a digestive enzyme that is thought to help prevent blood platelets from sticking together or building up along the walls of your blood vessels – obviously a well-known cause of heart attacks.
- Salmon – excellent source of fatty acids, especially omega-3s, some of the best anti-inflammatory substances out there.
- Bone broth – I love to eat this when I'm feeling a bit under the weather and it helps particularly with colds.

I try and make sure I have a proper breakfast – see the next few pages for some of my go-to faves that never let me down. For lunch

I normally keep it simple as it's just me if I'm at home and baby Paul is having something I've already prepared for him. I try and roast a chicken once a week – I just put it in the oven with chicken stock, carrots, onion and garlic, and roast it until it's cooked through and nice and brown. That means I have something to pick at and also use for making baby Paul a casserole. I love a chopped salad with breast meat or I mix it with some brown rice for a filling but healthy lunch.

Next up are some of my favourite recipes for me – they're healthy and contain all the food groups I know are good for my gut and for new mums who want to eat well. They're also great because baby Paul can have most of it whizzed up in the blender, so I know he is eating well too.

Breakfasts

The classic avocado and egg on rye

Serves 1

1 slice rye bread
½ avocado
1 tsp coconut oil
1 organic egg
½ tsp paprika
½ lemon
Sea salt and black pepper

- Toast the bread and mash up the avocado in a bowl, using a fork. Spread the avocado over the toast with a knife.
- Heat up the coconut oil in a frying pan and crack in the egg. Sprinkle with paprika and fry until it's done the way you like it. Use a spatula to remove the egg from the pan and to top the avocado with it.
- Squeeze over some lemon juice and add salt and pepper to taste.

Eggy toast and spinach

Serves 1

2 organic eggs
2 slices gluten-free bread
1 tsp coconut oil
Large handful of spinach
Tamari
Sesame seeds

- Whisk the eggs, in a bowl.
- Lightly toast the bread and dip it in the eggs, coating each slice evenly.
- Heat the coconut oil in a frying pan on a medium to high heat and add the toast. Cook until golden on both sides.
- Transfer the eggy toast to a warmed plate and throw the spinach into the pan. Cook for about 30 seconds until wilted.
- Serve the spinach with the eggy toast and season with tamari and sesame seeds as liked.

Deluxe porridge

Serves 1

40g gluten-free organic oats
250ml almond milk
Pinch of Himalayan salt
½ tsp ground cinnamon
½ avocado, sliced
Handful of nuts and seeds of your choice
Handful of organic chopped dried fruit of your choice
1 tsp honey

- Simply combine the oats, almond milk, salt and cinnamon in a saucepan and stir for 5 minutes on a medium heat until creamy (you may need to add some water if it's too thick).
- Transfer to a serving bowl and top with the avocado, nuts, seeds and dried fruit. Drizzle over the honey.

Breakfast goodness bowl

Serves 1

5 asparagus spears, trimmed

5 cherry tomatoes

Olive oil

1 organic egg

50g cooked quinoa (see package directions)

½ avocado

Handful of fresh rocket

½ lemon

Sea salt and black pepper

- Preheat the grill to a medium heat and assemble the asparagus and cherry tomatoes on a griddle pan. Drizzle with oil and season to taste before placing under the grill to cook for approximately 7 minutes, turning halfway through.

- Meanwhile, fill a small saucepan two-thirds full with water and bring to the boil before cracking in the egg. Turn down the heat and simmer for 3–4 minutes, or until cooked to your liking.

- Spoon the quinoa into a warmed serving bowl and add the avocado, rocket, grilled asparagus and tomatoes. Top with the poached egg. Finish with a squeeze of lemon and sprinkle with salt and pepper.

Mid-morning snacks

Some quick suggestions:

- Rye bread topped with natural mixed nut butter, banana, and strawberry slices and maple syrup.
- Cinnamon porridge with yoghurt, apple slices, chopped walnuts and honey.

Beetroot and white bean dip

1 cooked bulb beetroot
1 carton cannellini or butter beans, drained
Handful of fresh parsley
1 clove garlic, crushed
1 tbsp extra virgin olive oil
Juice of ½ lemon
Sea salt and black pepper

- Simply combine all the ingredients in a blender bowl and blend until smooth. Trasnfer to a serving bolw and serve straight away with raw vegetable crudités.
- Keeps, covered in clingfilm, in the fridge for 3 days.

Lunches

Crispy bacon lentils with poached egg

Serves 4

> 4 tbsp coconut oil
> 4 bacon rashers
> 300g puy lentils
> 1 tsp dried oregano
> 1 tsp dried basil
> Pinch each of sea salt and black pepper
> Splash of apple cider vinegar
> 4 organic eggs
> 2 handfuls of shredded spinach
> 4 tbsp olive oil

- Start by making the bacon lentils by heating up the coconut oil in a large saucepan. Cut the bacon rashers into thin strips – I use scissors for this bit as it's so much easier than using a knife – and add them to the hot pan.
- Fry until lovely and crispy – this usually takes about 8 minutes.
- Rinse and drain the lentils in a sieve and then add them to the pan with 500ml water, oregano, basil, sea salt and black pepper before bringing to the boil. Once it's boiling, turn down the heat

and simmer until the lentils are tender. This should take about 15–20 minutes. You might need to add in extra water halfway through, so check every now and then that they aren't drying up and needing more moisture.

- If there is any excess water, make sure you drain it off and give it all a good stir. Put to one side while you make the eggs.

- Heat some water in a large frying pan with a splash of vinegar until boiling. Carefully crack the eggs into the pan, turn down the heat and let them cook for about 4 minutes.

- Serve up the lentils on warmed serving plates, top each one with an egg and sprinkle on the shredded spinach. Finally, dress with olive oil, black pepper and sea salt and then you're good to go!

Salmon salad

Baked salmon is one of my favourite go-to light lunches and it also means that I can blend some up for baby Paul too if it's just us at home. You can't beat it for clean eating and packing in loads of healthy fats too, which are important for me when I'm still breast-feeding. I absolutely love eating oily fish and it's packed with skin-loving goodness. As well as the avocado, there are walnuts in the salad, which are great for maintaining a healthy and happy body. We have become scared of fat but I'm a great believer that good fats are essential for shiny hair and bright skin.

This is perfect for busy, time-poor mums as it only takes 15 minutes to make, but tastes amazing and leaves you feeling full and healthy.

Serves 2

2 x 150g boneless salmon fillets
1 lemon, halved
4 handfuls of fresh rocket
½ cucumber, chopped
2 avocados, sliced
½ fennel bulb, trimmed and thinly sliced
Handful of crushed walnuts
2 tbsp olive oil
Pinch each of sea salt and black pepper
Dried chilli flakes, to taste

- Preheat the oven to 180°C/Gas 4. Meanwhile, place the salmon fillets in a baking dish. Squeeze the juice of one half of the lemon on top and put the dish in the centre of the oven to cook for about 12 minutes.

- While you are waiting, prepare the salad by tossing the rocket, cucumber, avocado slices, fennel and walnuts in a salad bowl.

- In a small glass, mix together the olive oil and the juice from the other half of the lemon, and pour over the salad. Toss until all the salad is coated in the dressing.

- Remove the salmon from the oven and plate up with the salad. Sprinkle with sea salt, black pepper and chilli flakes to taste.

If you want to change this up, you can substitute the salad for a roasted vegetable medley:

1 small sweet potato
½ courgette
1 small red pepper
½ red onion
1 tbsp rapeseed oil
Sea salt and black pepper
1 garlic clove, peeled

- Peel and chop the sweet potato, and chop the courgette, red pepper and onion before placing them all in a baking dish. Drizzle with oil, season with salt and pepper, and add the garlic clove. Roast in a preheated oven at 180°C/Gas 4 for 40 minutes.

Green bean, broccoli and feta salad with pine nuts

Serves 1

Pine nuts
Olive oil
Juice of 1 lemon
Sea salt and black pepper, to taste
200g green beans, trimmed
200g tenderstem broccoli, trimmed
100g feta, chopped

- Fry the pine nuts in a dry frying pan until evenly toasted.
- Mix together the olive oil, lemon juice, salt and pepper in a small glass.
- Bring a saucepan of water to the boil and add the beans and broccoli. Reduce the heat and simmer until the vegetables are tender but still have bite.
- Drain, transfer to a serving bowl and mix in the dressing.
- Sprinkle with chopped feta and pine nuts to serve.

Dinners

Healthy burgers

This is perfect for a summer BBQ or a healthy alternative to a take-away burger, without all the grease and fat. These burgers are made with 100 per cent organic lean pork mince, which is a healthier alternative to beef, as it's really high in protein but naturally lower in fat. It's also rich in B vitamins, which are crucial for keeping your energy levels up and nourishing your body from the inside out.

I have always loved the combination of pork, apple and sage, and these burgers are so quick and easy to make. Instead of wedging them between bread buns, try serving them with roasted sweet potatoes and you won't look back. As with so much of the food I make for me and Paul at dinnertime, I can have the leftovers for lunch the next day and whizz some up in the blender for baby Paul.

Serves 2

150g sweet potatoes
1 tsp coconut oil, melted, plus extra for frying
1 apple
2 garlic cloves, peeled
1 white onion, peeled
Bunch of fresh sage leaves

200g organic lean pork mince
1 tsp dried rosemary
Sea salt and black pepper
Greens of your choice, to seve (I like the bitter taste of rocket with
the meat juice)

- Preheat the oven to 180°C/Gas 4. Meanwhile, prepare the potatoes by scrubbing and chopping them into cubes. Place them in a baking dish, drizzle with coconut oil, sprinkle over the salt and pepper, and roast in the centre of the oven for 40 minutes.
- Twenty minutes before the potatoes are ready to take out, make the burgers. Simply remove the core and grate the apple, finely chop the garlic, onion and sage, and add to a bowl with the pork mince, rosemary, salt and pepper.
- Mix together well with a spoon so the whole mixture is well combined and then form into burger shapes by rolling and flattening out the mixture a handful at a time.
- Heat up the oil in a frying pan and fry the burgers for about 5 minutes on each side until brown all over. You might want to cut one in half to check it is cooked through – if they are a little bit pink then give them a few minutes longer in the pan. Serve with the potatoes and greens of your choice.

Gaynor's spaghetti bolognese

Serves 4

3 tbsp olive oil

2 celery sticks, trimmed and chopped

Handful of fresh parsley

Handful of fresh basil leaves, plus extra to serve

1 onion, peeled and chopped

2 carrots, trimmed and chopped

3 garlic cloves, peeled and finely chopped

400g organic beef mince

2 x 400g tins chopped tomatoes

400ml chicken stock

2–3 bay leaves

1 tsp oregano

50g spaghetti

- Heat the olive oil in a large, high-sided frying pan over a medium heat and add the celery, parsley, basil, onion, carrots and garlic. Leave to sweat until softened.

- Add the mince and fry until it is all browned, draining off any excess liquid. Keep the heat on high until everything is coloured.

- Stir in the chopped tomatoes, chicken stock, bay leaves and oregano. Turn the heat right down and slow-cook for 3–4 hours, stirring occasionally, until you have a rich, thick sauce.

- When the sauce is ready, cook the pasta according to the packet directions, or make courgetti and serve with fresh basil.

Lemon sole and fennel

Serves 2

Juice of 2 lemons, plus some wedges to serve

2 tsp olive oil, plus extra for frying or use coconut oil

Small handful of fresh tarragon

2 sole fillets

1 fennel bulb, trimmed

½ onion, peeled

6–8 radishes, trimmed

Sea salt, to taste

- Mix the lemon juice and olive oil with the tarragon in a small bowl.
- Finely chop the fennel, onion and radish, and stir them into the taragon dressing.
- Heat a non-stick frying pan and add either some olive oil or coconut oil.
- Place each fillet skin side down in the pan. Fry for 2 minutes on each side.
- Spoon the fennel salad onto plates and top with the cooked fish. Season with salt and serve with lemon wedges.

Curried carrot and red lentil soup

Serves 4

1 tbsp coconut oil

1 white onion, peeled and finely chopped

1 clove garlic, peeled and finely chopped

1 tsp curry powder

5 carrots, trimmed and finely sliced

100g red split lentils

475ml vegetable stock or chicken bone broth or water

2.5cm ginger, peeled and minced

Sea salt and black pepper

Toasted seeds, freshly chopped parsley or corriander and rye toast to serve

- Heat the coconut oil in a large pan with a pinch of salt and throw in the onion, allowing it to cook until softened. Add the garlic, ginger and curry powder and sauté for 2 minutes.

- Add the carrots, red split lentils, soup, broth or water and black pepper. Bring to the boil for 10 minutes before simmering for around 20 minutes, until softened. Add in more water if you prefer a runnier soup, but keep as it is if you like it more rustic!

- Use a hand blender to blend the ingredients until smooth. Reheat and serve up with toasted seeds and freshly chopped parsley or coriander, plus the rye bread.

Thrown-together dishes

These dishes are just what they say on the tin – they're thrown together and perfect for when you're in a rush but still feel like something healthy. These are just starting points, really – with a little bit of confidence in the kitchen, you can find your own thrown-together dishes just as imaginative and tasty as these ones!

- Wild salmon with organic, locally grown new potatoes, peas, hummus and mixed salad.
- Sprouted bread, hummus, tinned salmon, cucumber, tomato, red onion, fresh rocket and black pepper.
- Avocado and sourdough with poached egg and pancetta.

Weaning

Giving you a window into how I eat and why I choose the diet I do sort of leads me on to how I weaned baby Paul. As a family we choose to eat fresh, organic foods and I cook from scratch for all of us, including the baby.

The first thing I would say about weaning is that although I read loads of different advice on when to do it, what to give him and what was best for him, I was in absolutely no rush to start. Although he was a relatively normal size when he was born (just under 7lbs), he has always been a really hungry baby who fed well and it didn't take him long to chunk up after he was born – he has always had cute chubby legs and arms. He's never been a skinny baby and I have never worried about his weight, so for me, our easy breastfeeding rhythm worked well and wasn't something I was looking to change in a hurry.

Again, I know everyone is different but, as with the breast-feeding, the weaning was something I wanted to do my way. It was also another key area where everyone was happy to tell me the way I should do it! I can't tell you the number of times I heard the phrase,

'Ahh, I bet you can't wait to start him on baby rice so he sleeps through the night?' Every time I heard that I just thought, 'What are you talking about? No, I don't want to give him rice just because that's how everyone else has done it.'

So I bought loads of books and took a bit from each, as well as thinking about my Crohn's and possible trigger foods. Taking my lead from my own diet, I decided that I was going to start with homemade fruit purées and yoghurts. For me, the rice was out – I have never been obsessed with getting him 'through the night' as you know (that's why at nine months he had still never slept the whole night!). I was more interested in introducing him to different flavours, textures and foods that he could easily process and that would keep him regular. I'm sure any mum who has Crohn's would understand wanting to give their baby a diet that was as healthy and clean as possible, not least as it would mean he could eat what I did and that would cut down on the amount of work that cooking two separate dishes every time would bring. Aside from the Crohn's, which baby Paul doesn't have, my big aim is to pass on a love of food and for him to be open to trying new textures and flavours. I don't want him to be a fussy or boring eater and I think the more I can get him to try when he is young, the better.

To start with I relied on making up my own recipes for baby Paul by playing about with flavours and different foods. I suppose my love of cooking first started when I got together with Paul. Our date nights out eating in restaurants and going for drinks were fairly short-lived – we had about 16 weeks before I was off the drink and being careful about things like sushi and shellfish! The more pregnant I was, the happier we were to stay in and so I suppose I naturally started trying to get better at recipes and trying new things. It's lovely to have people to cook for (something you just don't have as a single girl) and now I have two hungry boys who love food, it's making me try loads of different stuff I would have been too scared to try before. They both eat absolutely everything, so they are easy to please!

At the start of giving baby Paul solids, I kept it clean, light and simple – mainly fruit. I will never forget his little face when he tasted what was on the spoon for the first time; he pulled the funniest face and looked really shocked! He soon got the hang of it and I'm really proud that he has always tried and enjoyed everything I've given him. I actually can't think of anything he hasn't eaten or that he has spat out in protest – he will give anything a go.

It was a big step for me, introducing solids and knowing that he was not totally reliant on me for food any more – it was definitely more of a milestone for me than him. There was something so grown up about seeing him sitting all strapped into his highchair. Gone was that little baby who couldn't hold his head up for long, or who had just learned to roll over. My big boy was sitting up, holding a spoon and raring to go!

Starting out – food for beginners!

As I said, I started in a really low-key way, as I didn't want to overwhelm him. His first food (and still one of his top favourite things) was pear. To make it a bit more interesting, I do the following:

- Steam a chopped pear and apple, and throw them in the blender with a handful of strawberries and a banana. I add a teaspoon of ground almonds, a teaspoon of desiccated coconut and a splash of flaxseed oil (which I was told was great for preventing constipation). I blend it all up to make the loveliest puree – it's delicious and creamy and we both eat it! I make a container of it to keep in the fridge and it's the perfect breakfast on the go if I haven't got time to make something from scratch first thing in the morning and we have to get out in a hurry.
- Early on he also got a taste for porridge. He loves it when I add banana, strawberry and steamed pear.
- He has always loved kefir like me and I make sure he has it every day. We drink it together first thing in the morning – it's our little ritual to start the day.

The next stage

Because Paul was so open to trying new things, we moved to the next stage quite quickly – when he was about seven months. It also helped that it coincided with his teeth coming through so I felt happier about giving him lumpier food. It is always a bit scary the first few times you feed your baby lumps. I was worried he might choke and something would get stuck in his throat, but he managed fine and I always had a beaker of filtered water by the highchair just in case.

I think there is such a short time for mums to have control over what their kids eat. Once they go to nursery and school it gets harder to keep on top of who gives them what and what sort of treats they're given. I know every mum is different, but while it's up to me I don't want him having anything processed or any refined sugars – biscuits and chocolate are out for now but that will change as he gets older.

Once he could handle the lumps, I made dinner for me and Paul and then put some, unsalted, into a bowl for baby Paul the next day that would keep in the fridge. It cut down on the cooking as filming for the show took over and work got more hectic.

Like most mums I started off doing the big cook off on a Sunday afternoon, with great intentions of freezing loads of portions that I could just defrost whenever I needed them. But the truth is that having a defrosting freezer bag of food in the bottom of your nappy bag isn't ideal when you're out and about! I found that if I was out he was often having boob to get him through and if I was in then it was just as easy to whizz up some purée. It's all trial and error really, and some days we are up and out so early that he just gets by on boob until mid morning – it all depends on what we're doing and how hungry he is.

For now I'm just enjoying the freedom while I still have it because I know that, as he gets older, he might start going through a fussy stage. I have seen it in my friends' kids and definitely in Nelly as she has got bigger – she certainly knows what she does and doesn't like! Her food choices and likes have changed and she likes a say in what she eats and does now. (She is just like Billie on that front, who gets cross if she doesn't get her tea and biscuits!)

I'm happy to give him as much variety as I can, as me and Paul love all sorts – I think it is important that he grows up knowing what he does and doesn't like, especially for when he's in nursery and beyond.

At the point of writing this, his mealtimes are pretty much like ours and so I make sure we all have breakfast together in the morning. At 9 months, his routine if we are at home for the day looked like this:

- At around 6–7am baby Paul wakes up (normally in the bed with us!) and has boob. I get up and leave the boys in bed for cuddles and play, and go downstairs to get some chores done before they come down.

- If it's a relaxed morning then we all come down together and he will play in the corner with his toys for a good hour while I potter around doing washing or catching up on emails. He is at his best playing on his own in the morning, before he fully wakes up and realises he wants to walk along the furniture all day long! After about an hour he will start moaning, which is my signal that he's hungry and to get cracking with breakfast!

- If Paul has time then we have breakfast together and I make them both the same – baby Paul's new favourite is scrambled egg and asparagus, which Paul loves too as it's nice and healthy.

- Paul goes to work and after his breakfast baby Paul usually has a nap for about an hour – I have cut out that mid-morning feed before his nap to try and get him used to going to sleep without the boob.

- Once he is awake I have chores to do just like everyone else – we might go swimming or up the high street, or to the supermarket where I put him in the trolley and give him something to hold to distract him as I go round with my list. I take snacks with me like carrot or bits of apple.

- Once we're home it's lunchtime and he will happily eat and then sit in his highchair for a bit if I give him a piece of orange to suck on and distract himself with. The other day he sat there while I prepared a whole dinner for me and Paul, just pushing a piece of orange around his highchair tray!

- Sometimes he has an afternoon nap, sometimes he doesn't! Some days it is hardcore and I think to myself 'You haven't slept for hours!' Those days are hard work and now he is more mobile he needs my full attention – those are the days when I get nothing done and the house looks like a bombsite. It is that classic thing where you start something and then leave it half done, but I try really hard not to beat myself up and accept that it's all part of being a mum.

- In the late afternoon I do my best to make him as tired as possible and, once Paul comes home from work, that's his job. It is play, play, play, and then quiet bath and milk time – and hopefully he will sleep! He usually sleeps until midnight so that means me and Paul can have an evening, if we aren't asleep by 9pm!

Baby Paul's favourite breakfasts

- Asparagus cooked in coconut butter with three or four cherry tomatoes. Then I poach an egg in boiling water for three minutes with some vinegar. Meanwhile, I blend the asparagus and tomato (but not too much now he is older and needs to get used to texture). Then I cut up the egg with a knife and fork, again so that it has lumps in it, and mix it all together – he absolutely loves it!
- Avocado mashed with banana and some strawberries on the side.
- Kefir and fruit.
- Egg and avocado – he loves eggs – hardboiled or scrambled with avocado and coconut butter and asparagus. Basically whatever I have in the fridge!

Bathtime with Mummy.

Cuddles with Auntie
Billie in the sun.

My little gummy bear finding his toes in Italy.

Majorca kisses: dressed for dinner but always time for a family picture!

First trip out in the Silver Cross.

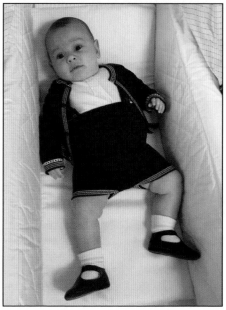

All dressed up for a day
of meetings in London!

Mummy and baby Paul getting ready to hit the town.

My two Arsenal fans (and a sign of things to come!)

Two Pauls in the pool – baby Paul showing off his swimming moves.

My all-time favourite picture – just look at those tummy rolls!

First taste of food – Mummy's milk and fresh pear.

Nanny Sue and her crew!

Already a little pro when it comes to the paparazzi!

The tea towel debacle – there's nothing you can do when they need to feed, even if you are live on TV!

Our first formal
photoshoot as a
three – my family
is everything to me.

On holiday in Sardinia with baby Paul
– a toddler now! I love the faces he
pulls – the one above is his classic pose!

Lunches and dinners

Now baby Paul is that bit older he basically eats what I do and my go-to recipies are anything by Annabel Karmel – we were introduced on *The Mummy Diaries* and baby Paul couldn't get over her food! Her 'My First Chicken Curry' gave me the confidence to try baby Paul on a mild korma and he absolutely loved it! Poor baby doesn't really have much choice as his daddy LOVES curry – it is literally Paul's favourite meal in the world, so baby Paul had better get used to it!

One of his favourite lunches that Annabel kindly shared with me was Sweet Potato, Pear and Broccoli.

Sweet potato, pear and broccoli

A well-balanced purée packed full of goodness, thanks to vitamins A and C, found in the fruit and veggies.

Prep time: 10 minutes
Cook time: 35 minutes
Makes: 4 portions
Great for: 6-9 months
Suitable for Freezing

15g butter

150g leek, chopped

250g sweet potato, diced

150g butternut squash, diced

200g pear, peeled and sliced

500ml water

80g broccoli, chopped

100g milk

50g Parmesan, grated

- Melt the butter in a saucepan. Add the leek, sweet potato, squash and pear. Gently sauté over the heat for 4–5 minutes. Stir in the water.

- Cover with a lid, then bring up to the boil and let it simmer for about 20 minutes until tender.

- Add the broccoli, cover and simmer for another 8 minutes until soft.

- Pour in the milk, then blend until smooth or your desired consistency using a hand blender. Stir in the Parmesan.

Baby Paul's other favourite foods include:

- Gaynor's spaghetti Bolognese (see page 201) – he has that without the pasta, just on its own with some cheese and he loves it almost as much as Paul does!

- He loves fish and I make sure I give it to him twice a week. He eats any white fish and seems to really enjoy it when I put it with asparagus. He loves salmon in particular and I poach it, and then mix it in with spinach and roasted sweet potato. To mix it up, I add sautéed garlic and onion.

- He really enjoys my mum's turkey meatballs with tomatoes. She makes it especially for him and keeps some in the freezer for when we pop over.
- He is quite keen on salad ever since I gave him some of a tuna and onion salad I'd made for lunch. I just put it in the blender and he ate the whole bowl!
- A surprise hit was when I made lemon sole with a fennel salad, which you can find on page 202. I wasn't sure how he would be with the fennel as it is quite strong but he loved it.
- He loves a mild korma and is now able to join in curry night!
- Something that is good for batch cooking is if I keep back the breast meat from my poached chicken and mix it with some kale and roasted butternut squash. I also use it to make a chicken, carrot and pea casserole that me and Paul have been known to share too once baby Paul has gone to bed. Since having him, I now totally get why so many mums talk about eating leftovers – there is something so nice about the mushiness of baby food!

Snacks

All mums know that you can NEVER leave the house without a snack. It's rarely about actual hunger and mostly a distraction technique! Baby Paul loves snacks – they are particularly great to keep him quiet in the car if he isn't tired, or in the trolley if we're in the supermarket and he is too hungry to shop. I often have pieces of apple and pear all cut up in Tupperware ready to go. He is a great fan (like his mummy!) of hummus and raw carrot – he also seems to like celery sticks too. He loves all fruit – especially a banana to squish in his highchair or an orange quarter, or some strawberries to chase round his highchair tray.

What equipment will you need?

You probably have most of the equipment for making your baby's food already, but here is a list of gadgets that I found handy:

- Sieve
- Ice cube trays for smaller portions when they are just starting out and tasting different flavours. (Don't start off by making huge batches of something they might hate!)
- Food processor
- Nutribullet
- Hand blender
- Freezer bags.

Milestones

Weaning baby Paul seemed to come at the same time as lots of other changes – in a way it felt like my little baby was disappearing.

He suddenly learned to roll over and sit up within weeks of each other, which was obviously an amazing moment but it also meant extra danger! Every mum out there will remember that moment you suddenly realise how hard it is when you can't leave your baby on your bed as you run around getting ready in the morning or while you nip to the bathroom and go for a quick wee! I soon saw what a lifesaver that had been and how difficult it was now I had to take him with me in case he rolled off the bed. It also meant that I couldn't leave him on the living room floor unattended in case he rolled into the fireplace.

The baby-proofing began right away: the plug sockets were covered, the cushions came off the sofa and were propped up against the walls in the corner where he played so that if he fell back when he was sitting up he wouldn't hit his head on the wall or skirting board. The Sky box wires were hidden under a blanket and we starting putting our cups of tea up high and out of reach!

There were equipment sort outs too – out went the lovely white baby gym with its hanging animals that he so loved, and out went the iCandy carrycot and in came the pram seat with straps that meant he could sit up more and see what was going on. He also started to hate his vibrating and swinging chair and spent all his time leaning forward and trying to escape on to the floor where he could get stuck in! These were replaced by the marvel that is the Jumperoo, where your baby can sit with straight legs (like in a baby walker) but jump up and down non-stop, surrounded by lots of hanging animals that make noises and sing. It's one of the best inventions ever as they are safer than in a bouncer that hangs from the door frame and you can move it to whichever room you're in so you can see them while they stay safely contained.

He started to get a bit heavy for the sling and, if he did go in it, he liked facing forwards rather than my chest so he could see what was going on. I also noticed that if we didn't get out for at least one walk a day in the pram, he would go stir crazy and would be really grumpy until I took him out. He loves to watch the world go by and he started to love playing in the garden. He would spend ages watching the leaves on the trees in his pram while I got a few bits done. Now he's crawling, those days are gone!

His baby walker has been a godsend too – he loves whizzing around in it and can now follow me around the kitchen like a racing driver. He is so quick now and it is a brilliant thing to put him in so he is safe but still feels like he is getting about. You have to watch him on a wooden floor though – he gets everywhere!

Getting Back Out and About

When it came to the pregnancy and baby Paul's first six months, I just went for it really and threw myself in at the deep end 100 per cent. Baby Paul didn't leave my side – and still hasn't, really. I genuinely didn't miss alcohol, I didn't miss going out, I didn't miss the Essex scene and I was so happy to knock it all on the head; I just didn't fancy it. I genuinely thought, 'Why would I want to be out in a bar when I could be at home with my lovely baby?'

I know it isn't like that for everyone, but I was in no hurry to leave him. I love feeding him, getting him down to sleep, eating dinner with Paul and cuddling up on the sofa to watch something – even though we both instantly fall asleep!

It's weird really because, if I am honest, there are some people who find me as a mummy quite hard to deal with in that I'm not out clubbing any more and I go out hardly at all, apart from for a family dinner or a friend's birthday. The truth is that – as I'm writing this, with baby Paul at nine months old – me and Paul haven't even managed a proper night out on our own with the baby sleeping over at someone's house so that we could have a few drinks and a sleep in the next day, or maybe go to a hotel. It hasn't happened mainly because, at this moment, he is still waking at midnight and 3am for a breastfeed and sleeping with us. There's also the fact that each time I expressed a bottle for him to have on the two occasions I had to go to work without him, he didn't even drink them, he preferred to wait for the boob when I got home. I couldn't believe it, it was like he has a sixth sense! I don't think he's ready as he's still so attached to breastfeeding, it would be too much for him to wake up at 3am in a strange bed and be given a bottle – I have a feeling he wouldn't be too happy about it! It also wouldn't be fair on whoever was looking after him. Before I leave him overnight I think he would have to be sleeping through at least, so that I didn't feel I was taking too many liberties. Right now, I can't imagine leaving him overnight until he's at least 18 months old, but I know things change so quickly with babies, so I might feel differently in a few months.

When we do leave him it will feel like a really big deal and will be more traumatic for me than him! Don't get me wrong, I have been out for a few girlie dinners locally and that has been great fun, but I will bathe and feed baby Paul and put him down before I go. Then I always make sure I'm back before the midnight feed, normally by 11pm in case he wakes early. It also means that I can't go overboard on the drink, as I will be feeding him when I get in.

On the drinking front, for the first six months after he was born I felt about drink like I had when I was pregnant: I didn't miss it, didn't crave it and couldn't think of anything worse. For me, the thought of drinking booze that would get into the milk of my tiny baby was horrific, especially when he was newly born; he seemed so delicate, even too much tea didn't feel right! Up until that six-month point not drinking hadn't been an issue as I hadn't left the baby to go out. I was feeding on demand and I hadn't thought about getting any booze in the house, mainly as Paul doesn't really drink so it wasn't something that was on our weekly shopping list.

I didn't really give much thought to how long I hadn't been drinking for, but I realised that by the time I did get back on it, almost a year had gone by without me having a sip. The old me would have thought that was ridiculous! But I didn't even notice.

As I've said earlier, I had my first proper drink when baby Paul was seven months old, which was only a glass of Prosecco and was hardly a wild bender! I feel I can relax more now he's that bit more self-sufficient –psychologically, I think I needed to know that he could sit up and was eating proper food before I touched alcohol. At the start he was so small and helpless, and I felt such a pressure (from myself) to do everything perfectly – my friends and family call me the 'earth mother'. I did ease up on myself once he started weaning and seemed more robust. It's that teeny-tiny stage where you worry so much and I did obsess about what he was getting from my milk. I was very strict with myself and wouldn't eat anything I thought might be bad or even risk a glass of bubbles. My friends all took the micky out of me, calling me a hippy, as he was on the boob the whole time and everything I ate was organic or green! It was all a long way from the days of takeaways and partying. Once he started weaning and could sit up and crawl, I felt it was a good time to give myself a break and ease up a bit.

I know a lot of people didn't expect me to do things the way I have. Some even think it's odd – maybe they thought I would have him and be back out on the town in a few months. But for me (and I know everyone is different), it wasn't about 'getting my old life back' or 'getting back on it' – I had a baby when I was fully wanting life to move forward, when my priorities were changing. I knew things would be different and I was ready to fully embrace that. Being there for Paul and my baby is my priority now: it's the family we're building and that is my focus. Obviously we still go out and see our mates, but I'm so knackered most of the time that I love just getting into bed for an early night!

I also think that the reality of life in Essex and being on *TOWIE* is that I had been doing it for such a long time, in truth I knew I wasn't missing anything really. Gone were the days where I wanted to be out seven nights a week, clubbing and checking out new bars. My real mates come round and have dinner and a chat, and if I want to meet them out Paul will stay in or my mum or Gaynor will come round and babysit for a few hours. I'm never far away in case he needs the boob and he doesn't even know I've gone. Me and Paul have managed the odd meal to our local Indian restaurant round the corner, which we love. It doesn't have to be a big, fancy night in London for us; we're happy to just have a few hours to ourselves to catch up.

I know I'm lucky that me and Paul agree on everything to do with what's best for our baby – it is as important to him as it is to me that baby Paul feels happy and settled, is breastfed for as long as he wants and feels secure and is given all the attention he needs. We are united and that's how I want it to be as our kids get older: if they ask one of us for something we will automatically check they have spoken to the other too – there will be no playing us off against each other. I want my kids to see us respect each other's opinions and thoughts and points of view. As a threesome we have had wonderful nights out at hotels, weekends away, lovely dinners and holidays, and Paul and me agree that, for now, we both want baby Paul with us all the time. It's not like one of us is desperate to be out without him and get away from him. He just comes too and we do everything as a family – it's the nicest feeling.

That said, I know it's important to try and make time for me and Paul as a couple – we both believe we can only be the best parents possible if our relationship is solid. We also need to remember we haven't been together for that long, even if everything has gone a hundred miles an hour! It's hard because we're doing the most important (and tiring) thing in bringing up a baby, but we're still in the early days of being us. By the time baby Paul is a year old, me and Paul will only have been together two years. Most people haven't even moved in together by that stage and we will have a toddler running around!

We do try and remember about each other as much as we can. While I'm the go-to person all week, by the time Saturday comes round I'm knackered and Paul will get up with baby Paul and take him downstairs to play, or out for a walk so that I can grab a few extra hours' sleep. As mums we are programmed to get on with it and ignore the sleep deprivation, but sometimes I just hit a wall and

I need to stay in bed and catch up on sleep. That's where it is great to have an extra pair of hands. I honestly have the biggest respect for all the single mums out there doing it on their own and never getting any time off; it's one of the hardest jobs and I can't imagine not having someone to share it with. Aside from the tiredness, it's also just the everyday worries that you are getting it right and sharing those worries.

Of course it can be hard to make the couple special time – baby Paul usually goes down at 7.30/8pm and once that's done I find it hard to keep my eyes open! We will often eat and Paul will say, 'Come and sit here and watch a film with me,' And the truth is that I just want my bed. Really, that's when I should sit up and spend time chatting but often, if we do try and watch something on TV, we don't stay awake long enough to get to the end of anything!

Holidays

Ahh, how my holidays have changed. I used to book my all-inclusive breaks to Vegas or Ibiza and dream of being on a sun lounger by day and sipping cocktails in a posh bar by night – not a chance of that now! Actually, I would often get home more exhausted from those girlie breaks due to all the clubbing and, ironically, I get more rest now when I holiday as a mum. There are many things that make the holiday vibe totally different with a baby and I wouldn't swap it for the world.

Packing

It used to be loads of pairs of heels, clubbing dresses and pool party outfits for a week-long break. My suitcase was bursting with stuff and I would get home not having worn half of it. Not any more. Now it's all about baby Paul, and if I'm lucky I stuff in a few bikinis, some shorts and the odd dress. My style is more pared down now as I have got older and I'm much more comfortable in manageable heels and smart bits and pieces that I can put together to make different outfits from. Since having baby Paul I also can't remember the last time I packed really big heels for going abroad – I couldn't imagine going down to dinner in a pair of towering stilettos pushing a pram. Gone are the long dinners, sat enjoying the sea views; now I'm often feeding baby Paul or pushing him up and down in the pram trying to get him to go off. Just like at home, when we are away he comes everywhere with us. He eats with us and then just sleeps in his pram when he's tired. He is used to sleeping with lots of noise and hustle and bustle so it works well for us. We basically have a nice dinner and then go back to the hotel to chill.

Though I would pack loads of cute little outfits for him to wear at dinner, I didn't really end up using many of those either. Because the aim was to get him to sleep before dinner so that we could eat in peace, I would dress him for bed before we went out, feed him and then get him off to sleep in his pram. This meant that I ended up putting him in white babygrows most of the time, rather than the cute romper suit and shorts that I had packed.

The flight

You suddenly become truly aware of all the dirty looks you have given passengers in the past who were travelling with crying babies – and you feel *really* bad! You know how you always look (usually at the mum holding the crying child) and think, 'Why can't you stop that baby crying?' The answer is that you really can't do much if they lose it on the plane. It is literally a mum's worst nightmare to have a baby that just wants to be anywhere but strapped into a plane seat, restricted, tired and grumpy. All the things you would normally do – walk in the pram, walking up and down to distract him – you can't.

That said, baby Paul has usually been really good on the flights we have taken and he has got used to it now, mainly as he has been on lots of planes in his first year. His first trip was quite long haul, involving a flight to Dubai, and I made sure we picked night flights that would tie in with his UK bedtime, and then we sorted out the time difference the other end. By the end of his first summer he knew the drill and the minute we took off he would have some milk and fall straight to sleep. The rhythm of the plane sort of felt like the car for him and it knocked him right out!

Flight tips with a small baby

- Where possible I tried to take night flights if they were longer than four hours as it meant I could breastfeed and then snuggle up next to him and he wouldn't know the difference.
- Make sure one of your bags allowed for hand luggage is devoted completely to the baby. Don't just stuff a few things into your handbag – make sure you take proper time to make a list and pack accordingly.
- If you think you've packed enough nappies, pack more: you can never have enough!
- A travel changing mat is essential for mid-air messy nappies.

- Blankets – bring a few as you will use them to lie your baby on, wrap your baby up in if the air conditioning is too cold and cover yourself if you are breastfeeding.
- A couple of plastic bags for emergencies.
- Wipes and hand gel so you don't have to keep getting up to wash your hands. You might be stuck in your seat and not allowed to be up and about, so have as much to hand as possible.
- Tissues.
- Socks for cold baby feet and extra clothes for layering.
- Favourite toys – preferably ones without music that would drive the other passengers mad!
- Bibs and a few changes of clothing.
- Pack each clean outfit in its own plastic bag so you don't have to take everything else out to find it – chances are you will need to locate it quickly!

What tan?

The thing that no one ever tells you is that you might choose to go somewhere hot, but you won't actually get to sit still in the sun for long enough to get a tan. That's the magic of going away with a baby – you spend all your time putting on sun cream that they hate with a passion, and if you're not doing that then you're in the shade with them for the hottest part of the day so they don't burn. Whereas before my only thought would have been to pick the hottest time, once we started planning holidays with baby Paul I knew it would make life easier for us to go at a slightly cooler time of year. So with the trip to Dubai we picked April as it wasn't so desert hot and there was a breeze. He spent most of the time in a nappy, or completely naked, which he loved! Even though baby Paul is dark like me and Paul, I was really careful about his sun exposure. But I always tried to let him have a roll around as the sun was going down so that he got his vitamin D – I think it is really important for general health and mood but also good to get his skin used to the sun too.

But it's important to say that this is just my experience. The advice from the NHS is to limit sun exposure in children under 30 months of age – see the guidelines on their website detailed at the back of the book for more information. One thing I would say is that your baby and toddler's essential wardrobe during the summer months should consist of lots of short-sleeved vests, comfy cotton shorts, and cotton bucket hats in every colour to protect their face and neck from the sun's rays.

The villa is not your friend once your baby can crawl

During our late-summer holiday, it became obvious that mobile babies are a whole other problem on holiday. It is a game-changer and means hardly any rest – you need to have eyes in the back of your head! When baby Paul was eight months old we went to Spain and stayed in a beautiful villa – with a marble floor! It is no exaggeration to say that I carried him around for the whole holiday, as it was just too dangerous to put him down. He had just learned how to sit up and was falling backwards a lot and losing balance like they do at that age. Even with all the cushions in the world, it was highly likely that he would fall back, miss the soft landing and crack his head. My top tip about travelling with mobile babies to unknown villas with hard surfaces and floors that aren't baby-proof, is to take a baby walker. That way you know they are contained and safe but they can still get around and give you a bit of hands-free time.

My post-baby holiday look is totally different and very pared down

Paul loves me most with a tan, freckles, natural lashes and my hair scraped up, which is just as well as that's the staple look now when I go away. It's something I battled with at the start as it was hard to still find time to do things that made me feel good about myself in the run-up to a holiday. In the old days I would have had my nails done, hair done, maybe sorted my lashes, but with a baby to juggle there truly isn't time. The one thing I have kept up since he was born is the treat of having my nails done – it is the one thing that helps me feel fresh after sleepless nights and before a holiday when I know I won't get time to look after them like I did before baby Paul.

I also dress differently when I am away

It isn't just that my style has changed, it's that I'm still breastfeeding, so I need to wear things on my top half that allow easy boob access. So gone are the cute playsuits with the long zips up the back that require a spare hand to release every time you need a wee (but you don't mind because they look super stylish), and in are tops that are easy to lift, with shorts or light trousers (dresses are also hard for obvious lifting reasons.) Now baby Paul is a bit older he has started to search for my boob when he is hungry, so that definitely puts the pressure on being able to feed him quickly, especially when out in public.

It has been an adjustment as I don't want to be a drab mum – just because I have had a baby it doesn't make me middle-aged and I do have to remind myself I'm still really young and able to dress for my age. I don't have to cover myself just because I have had baby Paul, and I especially need to remember that on holiday. In the summer when we were away I found a pair of cute hotpants I had packed on the off-chance I would be brave enough to wear them. I got them out and tried them on to wear down to dinner and I remember coming out of our bedroom and asking Paul if he felt I could pull them off. I said to him, 'Do you think I can wear these now I'm a mum?'

He looked at me and laughed, saying, 'You're only 25, Sam, not a hundred! Of course you can wear them, you look great!'

I think that's the other thing about having a baby: you automatically feel so grown up and like you have to put all your young ways behind you – for me that also meant looking at my wardrobe.

You will feel different in a bikini

Basically you have less time to worry about yourself, especially how you look in a bikini. For the first time in your life it will be the last thing you think about. I didn't struggle loads to lose my weight, so I know that I am lucky to be happy with where I am on the scales before baby Paul has turned one. That doesn't mean I'm 100 per cent where I want to be as I might be slim but I'm not toned at all. I just haven't given it any time and so running around in swimwear is a different experience for me.

I still over pack – but for the baby now. I used to spend hours lying out whole outfits for myself, complete with shoes and handbags, now I spend it all planning out baby Paul's day-to-night wardrobe. I always pack way too much and end up bringing a lot of it home, clean and unworn. How times have changed!

Three top tips

- Make sure you take a load of coconut butter with you. I use it for everything. When we were on holiday baby Paul got dry skin because of the heat and the chlorine. I just smothered him in the butter and it cleared up instantly.

- Always travel with a hand blender once your baby is on solids. Often restaurants won't be able to blend up their food to your requirements, especially if they have just started on solids and can't deal well with lumps, so it's best to go prepared.

- If they are under six months, try and take a bigger pram so that they have plenty of room to sleep. It will help them stay asleep while you are out at dinner and mean that you won't have to transfer them into a cot straight away (and risk waking them) when you get back to the villa or hotel.

Teething

I was warned repeatedly about this phase and how awful it can be, particularly as it can go on for the first two years, which sounds pretty grim! The first tooth can come through as early as three months or as late as after their first birthday, but baby Paul's first ones came through at six months. They say that they can have around 20 teeth by the time they are a year old and at nine months baby Paul had six teeth in total – three at the top and three at the bottom, and the back ones were coming through with a vengeance.

At the start we definitely got off quite lightly on the teething front. I guess you could say that he broke us in gently! The first teeth to come through were the bottom ones and, apart from a few sleepless and restless nights and red cheeks, he didn't really seem to suffer too much. He didn't cry much and certainly wasn't off his food or too out of sorts; he just got on with it really. There were some runny nappies and some gum pain with lots of dribbling, but nothing too awful that disrupted everything.

The top teeth were slightly more hardcore and they disrupted him far more than the bottom ones. I'm not sure if it had anything to do with the fact that they started to come through when we were on holiday. Perhaps he felt it more because he wasn't at home with all his familiar things around him, or perhaps he was just at a stage where he wanted me more anyway. But the upshot was that he was quite clingy and wanted to breastfeed much more – only I would do and that was that. In fact, I couldn't even hold him without him wanting comfort from breastfeeding and, for the first time, my nipples got really sore. I think it was mainly because he was feeding more often than my body had been used to, but also because he was that bit older, which meant he was sucking much harder than he did when he was a newborn. Plus there were teeth, which made a big difference when he wanted to feed constantly throughout the day and night.

It was tough and unlike his easy-going nature to cry so much, but he was in a lot of pain and it broke my heart not to be able to take the pain away from him. He just wanted to be on me the whole time and he started crying whenever I left the room. This was around the time that he came back into bed with us and sort of regressed a bit – he was feeding a lot through the night and waking every couple of hours and needing me to settle him. It is hard when you think you have moved to a certain stage and then something happens – like teeth or colds – to set them back. But they go through stages all the time and the key is to remember that nothing lasts forever, even if it is tough at the time, it will pass. Once the troublesome teeth came through, I did try again with the cot and getting him used to sleeping on his own. It's all swings and roundabouts really.

The top teeth were probably my most challenging time – mostly because he has sailed through everything else without any issues. There were three really bad nights once we got home from our holiday when he was nine months old, when he screamed all night and nothing could calm him down apart from being on me. He literally screamed all night long, and it typically coincided with Paul being away so I was lucky that Gaynor could come to stay. But lovely as it was to have the support in the middle of the night, it was hard because he just wanted to be with me all the time. During those three tough nights he threw up everywhere: all over the bed and me in the middle of the night, and that is a killer, changing the sheets in the middle of the night! But after the third night he settled down. Although he still wanted feeding throughout the night, he wasn't screaming, which was so much easier to handle. I realise now that the back teeth were also trying to make an entrance at the same time as his gums were so swollen.

It was around this time that a bit of separation anxiety began to creep in. It had been the case that if he was engrossed in playing with his toys or being held by someone else, he paid no attention to whether I was in the room or not; he was easily distracted and would play happily. But around nine months, and during the time the teeth were coming through, he started to get a bit whingey when I put him down on the floor and would crawl straight back over to me with his arms up, telling me he wanted a cuddle. If I sat away from him on the sofa, with him on the carpet, he didn't like it much and would come straight over to me, and if I left the room he would really cry. It is hard when all this starts, especially if your baby has always been happy to go to anyone and been really good at enjoying their own company and amusing themselves.

Like everything, there are lots of different attitudes to what is best and how to nip it in the bud while still making them feel secure. Obviously you have to leave the room or else you would never get anything done, so they do have to gently get used to it. I started by making sure I was only nipping out quickly to get something and would tell him in a very calm voice where I was going. Something like, 'Mummy's just going to the kitchen to get her cup of tea', or, 'I will be back in a minute, darling, I'm just putting the washing on'.

Now obviously I know that he doesn't understand what I'm saying – no baby is that advanced! But it's more about using familiar words and the right tone of voice, which should be both firm and reassuring. They look to you for their lead on how to cope with every situation, and if you seem calm and in control they are more likely to relax and not think it's a big deal. I always reassure baby Paul by saying, 'Mummy will be right back, darling.' The key is that you remind them that you always come back. It's the same with the cot and bedtime; you have to find that balance between letting them cry a bit but knowing you will be back. It's hard and it takes time, but they will get there in the end.

Teething tips

- Keep a teething ring in the fridge as the cold will offer immediate relief.

- Be prepared for all the rules to go out of the window. The pain seems to get to them worse at night and they will be unsettled and want cuddles.

- By day they will be overly emotional, whingey and nothing will feel right. They will want you close and, like baby Paul, they might want to be on the breast a lot more than you are used to. It is hard, but it will pass and they do get back to their happy selves.

- They might get temperatures. This is normal and there are many ways to help cool them down, but obviously a fever can be a sign of something more serious too so there's no harm in talking to the doctor if you are worried. I didn't go down the paracetamol route with baby Paul, but I did try some homeopathic remedies and also found Ashton & Parsons teething powder and Bonjela really helped soothe him.

- Be on hand for cuddles – sometimes that helps more than anything else.

Playtime

I have loved every single stage of baby Paul's first year, but once he could play and interact I really felt like we could connect on a different level. There is nothing more amazing than when he laughs at me doing something really silly or pulling a funny face. His favourite for a while was when I would put him on the carpet and do a forward roll in his direction, making lots of noise as I did it. He laughed so hard. You know that amazing sound of a baby chuckle when they get overexcited? It's the most magical thing and I love it so much. I do lots of impressions and animal noises, and have turned into that madwoman who sings nursery rhymes at the traffic lights or does a barking dog as we go round the supermarket. The things we end up doing to get a laugh are ridiculous!

He is so happy-go-lucky and he loves impressions, animal noises, Spanish songs and nursery rhymes. He laughs at most things and loves interaction, particularly when people chat to him and he babbles back. I talk to baby Paul all the time and point out things to him wherever we are. I like to think that even if he doesn't understand me, hearing my voice will help him develop curiosity and an interest in what is going on around him. He particularly loves me explaining what the animals are up to at the farm and doing the noises. He was an early baby babbler and I like to think that our little conversations have helped with that. He also really listens to Nelly's chattering too and tries to talk to her, which is cute and good for his development.

Everyone always says I'm lucky he is so good. I know I am blessed that baby Paul has a naturally calm and happy nature. But I am a pretty chilled person, so I like to think some of that has rubbed off on him. The truth is that I have put so much time into him, even when I know I could be getting on with chores. I would rather be on the carpet playing with him and showing him something new. We read books and play with toys a lot, particularly at the beginning and end of most days. I also have this thing about all my children speaking different languages, particularly Spanish. As a result, a lot of his toys (if they talk or play music) are in Spanish and if he does watch TV or cartoons on my iPad (like *Peppa Pig*) they are always in Spanish too. He actually isn't that interested in TV; he will look at it for five minutes or so and then go back to his toys or having a chat. He loves nature and animals – and Nelly!

I know that some people think I'm mad. I often hear that 'babies that young don't know the difference' but I believe they do . How else do children grow up bilingual unless they pick up on language and chat every day? I have been known to sing to baby Paul in Spanish – especially when I'm changing his nappy and he needs distracting! Paul agrees that it's a good thing to make baby Paul curious; as far as we're concerned it is all part of giving him the best we can as parents. We talk about this a lot: the fact that you have to be united as parents on the big and the small stuff. Manners and respect are so important, but the most important thing is to give them time. I'm convinced one of the reasons that he is such a good baby is because he has a nice calm home and he gets time and attention.

Play dates and activities

I have been to a few places in Brentwood with Billie and Nelly, but I won't pretend that I love them. Perhaps it's because baby Paul is at a bit of an in-between stage right now – crawling but not quite toddling around confidently – he feels too young to me to be crawling around when all the bigger kids are steaming around the place.

Baby Paul did go to all the baby groups from a really young age, but it has been less of a feature as he has got older and life has got more hectic. The one thing that we have done religiously is swimming right from when he was eight weeks old. Me and Paul are absolutely certain that we want all our kids to know how to swim and be totally confident in the water from the very start, so we have taken him to the pool every Wednesday afternoon. As a result he has no fear of the water at all – he dives right under without any fuss at all and loved the sea the first time he went in with Paul. He didn't care about the cold or the saltiness. He is so confident and it is so great to see him getting certificates and moving up in his classes. He has also always loved bath time too, splashing and kicking away – he was never one of those babies who cried when you put him into the water.

When he first started the swimming it was his thing with Paul – they used to go off together in the car for their little boys' trip out. It was lovely while they could do that but things have got so manic at work for Paul that I have had to take over. It is weird though; it's like baby Paul remembers all those early swimming sessions with Paul because even now, when we are on holiday, he always swims much better with Paul than with me. He will really kick his legs for his daddy in a way he just won't for me – maybe he just feels more confident in Paul's grip, maybe it's their early bond coming through – but whatever it is, I love seeing it. Just like I love how baby Paul's little legs go mad when Paul comes in from work – he gets so excited to see his daddy and it is the most heart-melting thing to see. There is nothing more attractive than a good daddy and with Paul I definitely lucked out.

We did the whole baby sensory thing, which baby Paul loved. It was a bit odd at first as you feel so self-conscious in those groups, singing songs and clapping away, but he got a lot out of it. We also started one-to-one Spanish lessons. We had this lady come round once a week with instruments and toys, and they just play in Spanish, doing numbers and the alphabet. She would chat away in Spanish and introduce new toys to him – I suppose if you are going to have a talking, singing ball rolling around and making noise then it's good to know that it's actually teaching him words in a new language! He loved it but, like a lot of new things you start off, it was quite hard to keep it going once work kicked in and we were filming for the new show.

We did also try Sing and Sign, but I have to admit that I didn't love it much – it's one of those classes much more geared towards babies but it didn't really work for us. I know lots of mums who say that it has really helped their babies communicate well, doing words and actions at the same time, but I was more of a baby sensory fan as it gave him more freedom. They put a big sheet down on the floor for all the babies to lie on and then use LED lights to twinkle around. Then all the toys come out and they get to touch and try out everything – baby Paul absolutely loved it. People often ask me if it was weird going to these classes when you've been on the TV. I suppose at the start some of the mums did recognise us. But once you get started you realise that motherhood is just a community for everyone and those classes are mainly full of first-time mums all obsessed with their own babies – there is no time to be interested in anything or anyone else to be honest.

The class I absolutely loved most of all was baby aerobics – it is the maddest thing because you take your baby and you have a mat and then you use the baby as a toning weight. So you pull your body in, make everything go tight, and then you will do squats and lunges using the baby as the dead weight. It's a proper exercise class (i.e. you sweat a lot) but what's great is that rather than leaving them in a playpen, you make the baby part of the routine and can keep them close. I was at a bit of a disadvantage as baby Paul was so much bigger than the other babies, which meant I had to work twice as hard as he was so heavy to lift! I properly ached and my muscles really hurt afterwards, as I had to be overly careful in case I dropped the baby!

Baby Paul loved it and spent most of the class giggling at me lifting him up and down and bending over him doing my leg raises. He just laughed so much and thought it was hilarious!

Favourite songs

We love singing together and I find it's a brilliant way to distract him in the car. In fact, eight rounds of 'Twinkle, Twinkle' is the best way to get him to sleep in his car seat if we are on our way somewhere and he hasn't dropped right off. He likes music a lot (again, probably picked up from various photo shoots!) and loves being sung to. Paul is less keen on it as he feels so self-conscious, but I get stuck right in, as does Billie, and Nelly loves a crazy dance half hour too. The favourite tunes as far as baby Paul is concerned are:

- 'Twinkle, Twinkle'
- 'If You're Happy and You Know it Clap Your Hands'
- 'The Wheels on the Bus'
- 'Round and Round the Garden'
- 'Incey Wincy Spider'
- The Spanish alphabet sung badly by Mummy

Toys

My big thing about everything play-related in baby Paul's first year was that I wanted him to learn to have an imagination. I remember being really young and loving my toys so much. I would make up voices and scenarios for them all – everyone had a story. They are some of my best memories – playing on my own in my room or in the garden – and I think you need to encourage it from a young age. You can never be bored as a child if you know how to make up games and really get stuck in to imaginative play with whatever toys you have to hand.

When it came to toys, I adopted the same less is more attitude than I did to cots and prams – baby Paul doesn't have hundreds of toys and the house isn't coming down with coloured plastic so that he never learns how to play properly with anything. He has fewer toys and we spend time getting to grips with them and making the most of them. I like to make sure he has a good selection of problem-solving toys, like coloured shape sorters and bricks, and then also has toys that are good for coordination, like balls, puzzles and cars he needs to push along. I love being like a big kid and putting on the voices and getting involved in floor play, and he plays at his best when I'm there showing him how to do things.

Getting Around

It is so hard but I try not to crowd baby Paul as he learns to find his feet (literally) and tries to push his own boundaries. Any mum will know that it takes a lot of willpower not to hover behind them, both arms out just in case they fall and hurt themselves, but you have to remember that they will never learn if they don't have the odd knock. Once he hit nine months old, baby Paul was all over everything – he learned to sit up quite early on and that was enough for about a month or so, but then the fast crawling started and then he was everywhere. He has always had sturdy, chunky legs and then loved sofa surfing or walking up and down holding my fingers for hours on end (that's a workout in itself!). Once he was on the go I had to have a little word with myself about not suffocating him. Sometimes they have to fall down to learn not to do it again and I love that he is fearless – we call him the Danger Mouse and it is the perfect name for him. It's so important to us that he has confidence – I think that's one of the best things you can give your child.

I think it might get harder as he starts to play more with other children, especially if they are bigger than him – I will definitely be keeping my beady eyes on how they are with him! That said, I know it is also important to teach him to be gentle with other babies if he is playing in a group situation. He is a great hair puller and that can hurt – I know from experience! Poor little Nelly has such fine hair and we have all been waiting ages for it to grow properly and not be wispy anymore. Then baby Paul came along and one of his favourite games is to pull it as she walks past – it's a wonder she has any left!

As he gets older one of the main things we will be concentrating on is getting him to share nicely. There is nothing worse than a child who won't let others join in and play with all the toys there. On a basic level, it must be so embarrassing if it's your child that won't give up the toy that isn't his! It's a bit early for all that yet but I know it won't be long until I have to face it. I think we will be quite strict about stuff like that – manners, sharing, sitting nicely and eating – they are all really important ways to teach respect for others.

Talking of baby groups, we are out and about so much that it's important to keep a bag packed with all his favourite and necessary things – it just saves so much hassle if it's all there in one place.

What's in baby Paul's nappy bag

What you need when you're out and about with a baby changes quite significantly as they get older. When they are small you pack to make sure you can cope on the run with any poo and sick issues mainly – so it's nappies and changes of clothing that take priority over toys and snacks. As they get older it becomes more about distraction and entertaining – though it's always about the nappy situation! I keep a bag packed with the essentials at all times and then add in/take out stuff depending on what stage he is at and where we are going. I have listed the basics below – the things you will need no matter where you are:

- Water Wipes – he has never had nappy rash, ever, and I think that is largely down to the fact I don't use anything with chemicals or scent on his bottom when I change him.
- Lots of nappies.
- Two white babygrows in case of general spillage or other accidents.
- Clean muslins.
- A shawl for feeding when out and about so you can cover up.
- A bib – not that I use them often. I'm more likely to tie a muslin around his neck to catch the food as it drops!
- Scented nappy sacks.
- Breast pads (not so much now, but certainly at the beginning when leakage was happening a lot).
- Toys and teething rings to chew on.
- Tupperware with ready to eat snacks.
- A bottle or beaker with filtered water.
- Coconut butter for dry skin – especially if you are abroad or it is really cold.

Mum and Baby Wardrobe

As I've mentioned earlier, my day-to-day look has totally changed since I had baby Paul but now he is older I'm trying to fit in some 'me time'. That is usually a manicure locally or asking my mum or Gaynor to have him so I can pop to London to get my hair cut and coloured. My hair remains my one real treat that allows me some quiet time. Sometimes I just want to scroll through other people's social media and catch up on what they are doing, and sometimes I fall asleep if the hair wash is particularly relaxing! Depending on time, I might also have some extensions to thicken it up, but since having a baby it is shorter and much more manageable because it is my actual length.

When I'm in London I also take advantage of a few hours off to do a quick clothes shop and stockpile some of my favourite make-up. My particular favourite brands are: Charlotte Tilbury, MAC and Chanel. My mummy make-up look has definitely changed from my single-girl vibe, and now speed and simplicity are key. My new thing is a pared back, dewy look with a golden sheen. Don't get me wrong, I still enjoy making an effort and dressing up, but I like my freckles showing through and everything generally looking more relaxed and feeling less 'done'. Paul is a huge fan of me wearing a simple ponytail and casual gear – which is really all I live in now, as it is so much easier with the baby. There really isn't much point being too smart as it only gets covered in spit and the rest, but that said I don't slum around in a tracksuit or sportswear all the time. I do think you have to push yourself to make an effort to look and feel nice – it certainly makes the tiredness more manageable if my hair and nails feel fresh and I feel nice about my outfit. I would hate to become frumpy just because I've had a baby and I don't believe in keeping clothes for 'best' or going out – let's face it, they would never get worn if I thought like that!

In terms of my overall look, lashes are obviously important because I don't have any of my own, but apart from that I'm really not massively bothered about how I look in terms of make-up. As a result, my everyday look is mainly high street with a bit of designer thrown in. I like smart and relaxed trousers from Zara and simple tops. I still haven't really got back into the way of dresses or skirts as they just aren't practical while baby Paul still wants to feed so often. I'm thinking that around Christmas it will be nice to glam up – it's my favourite time of year and me and baby Paul both have our birthdays then too, which makes it all the more exciting. We are two days apart so the celebrations will last for double the time now he is here. I suspect there will be some sparkly dresses or playsuits going on, particularly as Minnies goes so big on the whole party season and I will be online modelling for them in the run-up to Christmas.

(Billie not so much as she will be heavily pregnant – it was my turn with the bump last year, hers this year!) I can also imagine that poor baby Paul will be dressed up in all sorts – he has already been given a reindeer jumper and a Christmas pudding babygrow, and I suspect there will be more to come. Between that and his Arsenal football kits, he doesn't really get left alone! But the highlight will be the fact that me and him have matching kilts, thanks to my mum's Scottish boyfriend who had them made specially. I cannot wait to put them on together and get some photos in our purple skirts – they are proper, heavy-duty kilts and beautiful so it could well become my new fashion must-have!

My mummy wardrobe staples – summer

- Skinny jeans.
- Nice white T-shirts and vests.
- Crisp white shirts (buttons are great for easy access).
- Zara basic cotton stretch trousers in navy, khaki or beige.
- Cotton sleeveless tops.
- Shorts.
- Chanel espadrilles.
- Nike Flyknit trainers.
- Todd flats.
- Multiple pairs of sunglasses.

My mummy wardrobe staples – winter

- White polo necks.
- Smart suede jacket or knitted cardigan.
- Skinny jeans or skinny cords.
- Flat suede boots.
- Knitted jumper dress.
- Wool swing coat.

Favourite shops for daytime wardrobe

- **Zara** – What did the world do without this shop before it was here to save every single fashion situation? They always have one great staple piece, normally a nice autumn-to-winter coat, and I live in their smart linen trousers and capri pants in the summer with plain T-shirts, shirts or tops. Their jeans are amazing for throwing on with a smart jacket or day top if I am out and about with the baby. I absolutely love their Zara basic range and if you pair them with the right accessories, the simplest trousers and tops can look a million dollars. They also do great scarves and jewellery too.

- **Minnies** – I know it seems obvious to say, but me and Billie are fully committed to Minnies in every way and there isn't a thing for sale in the shop or on the website that we wouldn't wear. I own pretty much everything that I have modelled on social media and I love the clothes we sell – just as well I have a walk-in wardrobe, as there is so much choice whatever the season!

- **H&M** – Also great for the basics like jeans and tops, and their accessories and costume jewellery are fantastic too. I quite often find the odd smart going-out top or jacket in there and their winter season is particularly good.
- **The Outnet** – This is great for going-out bits and pieces that are a bit more glam that the usual day-to-day look I go for.
- **Uniqlo** – I love this shop for their quirky knitwear, T-shirts, polo necks and vests. I regularly go in and stock up on basics.

Baby Paul's wardrobe

I really thought I would go crazy when it came to buying baby clothes, but it turns out I am actually really simple and old-fashioned when it comes to baby Paul's wardrobe. There is a big myth out there that it is impossible to find nice clothes for boys and that all there is to dress them in are jeans and dungarees. I haven't found that at all and love buying boys' clothes as much as Billie enjoys buying the girlie bits for Nelly. You can find some really smart stuff out there in high street shops but I'm also a huge fan of online. Once you know what you like, clicking a button online from the sofa while the baby naps is the best invention ever!

Baby Paul's wardrobe is definitely a mixture of high-street shops and then I tend to shop online for special occasions, as some of the sites are slightly pricier. In terms of high street, I love the following:

- **John Lewis** – I am obsessed with the organic white all-in-one babygrows from here – they are so simple and soft on his skin.

I have been buying them ever since he was born and they wash up brilliantly (as long as I remember to separate my whites and my coloureds!).

- **Marks and Spencer** – I like to get some bits from M&S as they have really good-quality stuff that comes up nice and big and that will last him through a season. It also washes up really well.
- **Baby Gap** – I buy the odd bit in Baby Gap. I liked it when he was very small as they did nice all-in-ones in whites and greys.

Online baby shops

I will admit that I do spend more online than when I am in shops browsing; it is just so easy to drag all the cute clothes into the virtual basket and I get more excited when his clothes are delivered than I do with my own shopping – who'd have thought it!

With baby Paul, I know what I like and I don't really experiment too much as we like the classic look and I'm not massively into him wearing patterns, so most of his stuff comes from these websites:

- **Child's Play** – This website was established in 1990 and is based locally in Ilford. They specialise in stocking a wide range of designer clothes, footwear and accessories for newborns upwards. The labels they stock include Armani, Hugo Boss, Burberry, Dolce & Gabbana, Fendi and Gucci. This is where I splash out now and again on some staple pieces for baby Paul that I pair with high-street extras. I like to have a look on here particularly before a holiday now he is a bit older and he stays up a bit later for dinner. I like him to look smart for the evening and I'm working on his holiday wardrobe!

- **Children's Salon** – Another website that sells designer wear and really beautiful bits, especially for babies. They are really traditional and have lovely shorts, two-pieces and romper suits as well as some gorgeous knits and separates too.

- **Alex and Alexa** – This is a Swedish brand and is probably my favourite of all the online shops I visit. It specialises in classic bits with a twist, like a detailed collar or an unusual light print, smocked edging and velour fabric. I particularly love their babygrow range called Kissy Kissy, which is affordable luxury nightwear. I love the all-in-ones so much I still dress baby Paul in them during the day even though he is crawling around now. I also really love the brands they stock that do traditional takes on classics, like Rachel Riley – smart and crisp white shirts with piping trims worn with shorts.

- **My First Years** – Me and Billie decided to do a joint collaboration not long after baby Paul was born, and both Nelly and Paul have modelled for them. I love to wrap him up in his personalised robes and onesies, and his personalised bear fleece is adorable, as are Nelly's flora pyjamas – they both look so cute.

- **The White Company** – I used to think this brand was just for the house and candles, but then I discovered their baby section on their website and that was the end of that! This site is also brilliant for plain bits and a real luxury. I love their velour onesies and I use this company more for winter cosy items. The fabric is brilliant, washes really well and stays super soft.

- **Petit Bateau** – This French designer makes gorgeous little numbers for babies. They do especially beautiful onesies and I love the nautical stripe that is their speciality.

Funnily enough, Paul is the one who really loves shopping for the baby. He is worse than me when he gets going! As I mentioned earlier, the first time that he had baby Paul he took him to Harrods for lunch and then decided to buy him a cashmere tracksuit. It was beautiful but not exactly what most men would come home with on their first day in charge of the baby! I have to say, much as I love an online blitz, there is nothing like the joy of mooching around a classy West End boutique, and I especially love the ones on South Molton Street, where I also recently indulged in some cashmere goodies for the baby – I just couldn't help myself! I also like to get the big things, like his winter coat, from a trusted brand like Moncler. He looks so grown up in it and it will be perfect to see him through the winter. So although I know it is pricey, I would rather invest in an everyday essential like that than buyer a cheaper one and have to buy three of them.

I don't really buy from shops like Next or anywhere else, mainly as I find that they do a lot of denim for babies, especially boys, and I am not into that. I don't like jeans on newborns; in fact, I don't really like denim on babies at all, so we had to find a look that worked for him as he got bigger and outgrew the babygrow stage. Once he started trying to take his first steps, I felt he was that bit older and able to carry off proper clothes. I like putting him in little outfits, but all he wants to do is get around and so I don't want to put him in any clothing that is restrictive. Even with the white babygrows that I really love him in, once he started crawling I had to undo the poppers and tie up the legs around his waist so that it made it easier for him to crawl and not slip on the kitchen floor. It means his little knees take a bit of a bashing, but he is safer. In fact, indoors he is always in just a little vest so he can get around with speed and ease, and bare feet mean that when he climbs up against the front of the washing machine, he won't slip on the floor underneath him.

I would say that his style is quite classic really. People have said that I dress him like Prince George, which isn't deliberate. It's just the way I like him to look in crisp white and nothing too patterned or over the top, and I do love the more old-fashioned clothes as they have so much lovely extra detail like smocking. Me and Paul dress ourselves in neutral colours pretty much all the time, so it is only natural we would want to pick the same sort of vibe for our baby. I have never wanted him to wear restricting jeans and to stuff his little feet into Converse. I just think how uncomfortable I would be, never mind a tiny baby! It's fine when they are running around, but when they are babies, their bellies are so soft – why would they want waistbands digging into them? I'm always in my comfies in the house and I hate wearing uncomfortable clothes and make-up inside, so I imagine it's the same for baby Paul; I want him to feel chilled out when he's at home playing, and not dealing with a load of bunched up clothing slowing him down. I also really like babies to look like babies – there is plenty of time for them to follow fashion and look grown up, but that all-in-one stage is so precious and cuddly, I wanted to celebrate it for as long as possible.

That's one of the main things I have taken from this year: the time just flashes by and, before you know it, your little baby is a toddler and finding his own way. I am determined to hold on to the precious moments for as long as I can.

Saying that, we have got so much to look forward to as we approach the end of baby Paul's first year; he is already so different from my tiny baby I brought home from hospital. He loves playing, he loves his food (avocado is his favourite thing), he loves watching the leaves on trees, he loves causing chaos at Minnies and he loves his Nelly Noo. I can't wait for our first Christmas as a family and to celebrate his birthday too.

When we do light those candles I will be celebrating my happy, healthy baby, but I will also be celebrating the fact that me and Paul survived our first crazy, amazing year as parents. We have done things our way and that's the best piece of advice I can give: as long as your baby is thriving and you are surviving, you are doing it the right way for you and that's all any mum can do.

Epilogue

I know that it is really annoying to hear, but the truth is that I feel like the luckiest woman in the world with my little family to come home to every night. Meeting Paul and having our baby has allowed me to become a grown-up and I love every day as a mummy to our son. He is the biggest blessing and motherhood is everything I hoped it would be.

Don't get me wrong, there are good days and bad days, but I truly believe it is all about perspective – what works for one mum and baby doesn't always work for another and that is fine. Motherhood is the one area where people feel they can tell you what to do and it is just out of order and not helpful. There is so much pressure put on mums to conform and do things in a certain way, but you have to grow a thick skin and do what is right for *you*. I can't tell you the number of people who have asked me when I am going to stop breastfeeding as baby Paul is getting bigger – the answer is when we are ready. That has been pretty much my attitude throughout the first year: I am in no rush to do anything and will take my lead from my baby. My only aim is that baby Paul is happy and healthy and gets the very best start in life.

The one thing I have learned, and that I want you to take away from this book, is that if you are a happy mum and you have a happy baby then you are doing things the right way, because it is your way. It is an emotional and unpredictable rollercoaster with all that means – the highs are high and the lows can be the worst thing ever. There are hard days when you feel like you will never master it, when the baby won't stop crying and nothing soothes them, but those emotions and thoughts are so, so normal.

Motherhood is a massive adjustment but I feel happy and proud to be the parents that me and Paul have become. We are responsible for this baby and the boy and man he will turn into, and that is scary – but it is also the most exciting thing I will ever do. Being a parent is a million miles away from *TOWIE* and I love the fact that I don't get sucked into other people's dramas any more – I don't have time and I couldn't be less interested, and that's the way I like it.

Everything has been on fast forward since I met Paul, but when it comes to raising baby Paul, we will be traditional and together on everything. I know our parents are proud of how we have risen to the challenge and done things the way we want them, not how others tell us to. Our mums are particularly amazed at how we both took to it and I don't think anyone expected me to mother like I do – baby Paul rarely leaves my side and that's how I want it for now. The time when I will be waving him off to school will come round in a flash and I want to savour every single moment. I feel sad for people who wish away each stage because they are obsessed with getting them sleeping through or desperate for them to start walking – don't get me wrong, those milestones are important but it's the day-to-day stuff that I savour the most. Babies need you for such a short amount of time, so my advice would be to just enjoy it and don't get hung up on what they should be doing and when they should be doing it. Every stage is just that – something that will pass as they develop and move on to the next thing. Enjoy the moment for what it is and create new memories.

If anything, what I feel most lucky about is how close it has brought me and Paul. The other night, it was 10pm and the baby was still awake, his teeth were hurting and he had zero interest in sleeping. Every time I picked him up he wanted feeding and I was tired and sore. I just looked over at Paul and told him that he had to take him as it was too much. So he picked him up and took him downstairs and started the whole rocking and shushing thing. He held him tight, front facing in a rugby ball hold, and talked quietly to him. You know that scenario where they don't know what they want but nothing will do? Baby Paul was fully prepared not to settle for anyone until Paul got going. He held him tight and put on the overhead cooker fan and did his baby whisperer thing, rocking and talking quietly. He was so patient and eventually baby Paul dropped off and he slept on Paul's chest while he watched the football highlights.

I came downstairs to get a glass of water and saw them having their little moment and I felt overwhelmed with the thought that this was my very own family. Gone were my childhood dollies and the kitchen and pretend house, this was it: my two boys and our home. Sometimes I have to pinch myself that it is real.

Good luck with it all – and remember: if in doubt, follow your gut. It worked for me and I wouldn't change a thing.

Love, Sam x

Afterword:
My Toddler & Me

I started working on this book when baby Paul was six months old, and those early (sleep-deprived!) days were all-too vivid. We were still very much in the 'baby stage': he was chubby with baby rolls around the tops of his legs (and those little creases I loved so much!), he breastfed throughout the day, preferred to sleep on my chest than go in his cot, and was still dressed in cute white baby-gros. We were also experiencing a lot of first-time milestones, having just been on our first proper holiday as a family of three, and baby Paul had started to roll over and had tasted his first solid food. At that point, I was so strict about what he could and couldn't eat that people used to joke he was my little vegan baby! It feels like such a long time ago now – I look back at those pictures and think: 'Where has my newborn baby gone and how does time go so fast?'

That first year was a whirlwind, and like most mums I do often sit back and think: 'Wow, we survived!' It was the most intense, wonderful, exhilarating and exhausting year of my life, and I wouldn't change a single thing. I didn't leave baby Paul's side during that time (I still haven't left him overnight yet and he is 18 months old), I breastfed on demand and we co-slept. It was important to me and Paul that our baby felt secure and that he knew that he was the centre of our world – I feel so proud we achieved that.

But when he turned one I told myself (and Paul) that things were going to change slightly and that I was going to put a bedtime routine in place. Paul was not keen, he loved the baby being in bed with us and having him near so we could see and hear him, he also hated it when baby Paul cried (he always has and still does anything to avoid it!). But my mind was made up. I had been happy to do whatever the baby needed, but in the back of my head his first birthday was always going to be the point he went into his own room and his own cot; he was ready and I was definitely ready. Don't get me wrong, I found it so hard to think of him next door on his own, but I was determined and once I had made up my mind, I decided to get some advice on making it as stress-free as possible.

I knew the time had come for his own cot, as baby Paul wasn't sleeping that well and kept tossing and turning (as well as taking up the whole bed!). He would wake himself up sniffing for milk, which meant he was feeding throughout the night – it wasn't great for him and it was getting uncomfortable for all three of us. The night feeding also meant that he wanted more boob in the day, and I felt like we had taken a few steps backwards. So, three days after his first birthday, I devised a new bedtime routine that I hoped would mean he started sleeping in his own bed without too much stress, and then I just put it into place.

I had been told the best thing was to do something different but not totally new, in case it was too much change for the baby. So that first night, I bathed him and, rather than getting into my bed and feeding him like I always did, I brought him downstairs and gave him boob while he watched *In the Night Garden*. Once we had done that, I went back upstairs, put him in his cot and zipped him into his sleeping bag. I knew the key was to be in and out as quickly as possible while reassuring him, so I laid him down on his back, kissed him, told him I loved him, and then left and shut the door behind me. I made sure the room wasn't completely dark by leaving a small, faint nightlight on.

I don't know what I expected but I was prepared for a battle – after a whole year in our bed, he was probably going to be fuming with this new arrangement! Paul was anticipating the worst; in fact he arranged to stay at a hotel round the corner on standby, just in case it all got too much. He didn't want to go too far in case I needed him, but he also knew that he wouldn't be able to stand the crying and would want to go in and pick him up, which would not have helped!

Baby Paul cried for 10 minutes so I went in, picked him up and gave him a cuddle, then I put him back down and left. I wasn't in the room any more than 30 seconds, just long enough so he knew I was there. He cried for another 10 minutes and then he fell asleep – the whole thing took 20 minutes, I couldn't believe it! After a whole year of being in the bed with us, that's all it took! The second night it took 10 minutes and the rest, as they say, is history.

Now he goes down at 7pm and sleeps until 7am; we often get up before him! My only advice is to wait until they need the change – baby Paul was so ready and I know I could have introduced the routine to him at six months and he would have been fine, but we wanted him in the bed with us. But I could tell when he had outgrown it and was desperate for sleep (we all were!). It should always feel right for everyone or else you won't keep to it or feel comfortable.

There was a slight hiccup when we went to LA to film *The Mummy Diaries* and the baby slept with us in the bed, so when we got back to the UK it took a whole week to get him back in his routine, which I expected, to be honest. They say you should get back into it the first night you are home, but we all felt terrible. He suffered so badly with jetlag and I didn't have the energy to even try and force the routine. It took me two weeks to feel normal again as I was getting up at 3am with the baby – I had to suck it up and do what the baby wanted as he didn't know what time of day it was. After a week, I did the routine again and he cried a bit on the first night but that was it. Even the recent house move hasn't disrupted him – the first night he fell asleep after 10 minutes.

As he has grown older we have fallen into a good sleep routine and now he also has an afternoon nap at midday. We are usually out and about but sometimes it can be two hours. Like with all things relating to babies, there is no magic answer, but the key is routine and consistency. It's also about being confident that what you are doing is right for you all – that will help you not to give in. I don't feel bad because I know what's best for baby Paul.

I suppose the same thing applied to the breastfeeding, which stopped naturally when baby Paul was 17 months old. For the last month or so it was definitely just comfort for the baby, because I didn't actually feel my boobs filling up any more after he had fed. There was no big moment, it was a bit like the bedtime routine. I decided one morning to do something different because I knew it was coming to a head. Baby Paul was getting frustrated with me towards the end because there wasn't enough milk, I could feel him getting stressed as things had changed and he didn't know why. I thought that giving up the breastfeeding was going to be the most traumatic things for him – it is no exaggeration to say that the boob was everything to him. For me, it is something I am so proud of – I know how lucky I am that it worked out for us and was one of the most rewarding aspects of early motherhood. I loved every second, but it was never going to suit me to keep doing it until he was three or four years old. Each to their own, but he is so big now and I know he doesn't need it. It was the right time for both of us so, again, I just adapted the routine.

Normally in the morning I would get him out of his cot and he would be searching for milk so we would sit on the sofa and cuddle and feed, but one morning I thought I would try something different. I went into the kitchen and got him some water in his cup and gave him a biscuit before his breakfast to distract him. Baby Paul didn't look for a feed and then started to play with his toys, then he had his breakfast and we got dressed and suddenly it was lunchtime and before I knew it, it was bedtime. At that point, we had stopped the pre-bed feed because there wasn't enough milk, so I was bathing him and then putting him to bed. It just stopped and suddenly we had gone 10 days without any feeding.

I did notice that I had to wear tops that didn't show my chest or else he was all over me and searching for boob, but, other than that, it was all quite simple. I think it also coincided with me becoming more relaxed about his diet. I am a lot less stressed now, so if we are out I will look at the kids' menu and see what the best option is for him, whereas before I would have just said no and given him boob. When he was younger I was obsessed with him eating only pure produce – when they are little their tummies are delicate so I wanted everything to be perfect – but now he is much more robust. He still eats healthily and organic – but I will give him a chip if we are out and he can have a biscuit. He has sprinkles (little vitamins and minerals for babies) every day and he drinks lots of water and loves it. He's never ever touched juice and that's the way I want to keep it. My theory is that he's never tasted it so he doesn't know what he's missing.

We keep a healthy fridge in our house. Breakfast is organic porridge oats already crushed up with goat's milk, almonds, coconut shavings and some fresh bananas, strawberries and honey on top – it sets us both up for the day – and on Fridays we have jam on toast and sing the jam on toast song! He has a mid-morning snack, he's obsessed with bananas and will point at the side for one. Lunch will be leftovers – like a lamb roast with greens all blended up, not so it's smooth, but just so he doesn't choke. He had chicken noodle soup the other day and tried to feed himself, he also loves a mild curry, homemade chicken goujons, and cucumber – he's very open-minded and I try to mix things up so he gets a variety of food. I am convinced it's also because I ate well when I breastfed him, so his palate is quite sophisticated. He has, however, inherited Paul's sweet tooth and he can hear a biscuit wrapper a mile off and will point until you give him some! He also knows the difference between the baby stuff and the real deal, he's having none of it if it's a baby organic rice cake over a proper biscuit!

The way I see it is that I've had the hard bit upfront when he was tiny but I do think that I've made the next stage easy for myself – I know some of my friends thought I was mad having him in the bed all night and having my boob out all the time! But now, he's 18 months old and sleeps through the night, doesn't have a bottle, doesn't have a dummy or a comforter, and he's happy and confident. Other mummy friends are thinking about how they can take all those things away from babies his age, and I am done, really.

In terms of getting back to work, I do leave him for longer now and haven't really had the clingy stage, but thank God for FaceTime! No matter how long I'm out for, even if it's just an hour, I always FaceTime baby Paul at least once, just to see his little face. However, if I have a day out at work and Paul, my mum or Gaynor have him, he will be funny with me when I get home and he will avoid me, like he's punishing me and then he puts his arms up to the person who has had him that day. It makes me feel awful. I know it's developmental and totally normal but it is a blow! I don't like to disappear so I always say goodbye properly, so he knows where I am all the time. I say goodbye in a very upbeat way and do it quickly. I tell myself he is more independent now and I do feel much happier leaving him, but I can't wait to get back to him.

The truth is that, with your first baby, you overthink everything and you want to be perfect, but there is no such thing. Every way is valid and every mum should do what is best for her. I look at Billie now with two kids and I can't imagine it! Immediately after having Paul I said I wanted another one, but I am enjoying every stage so much and this toddler phase is so much fun. Now I'd say that two to three years would be a perfect age gap so they can be in the same school. I don't want to leave it too long as I feel we are in the swing of things and another baby wouldn't be too much of a shock.

Watching baby Paul with baby Arthur has been lovely and convinced me he will be brilliant with a little brother or sister. He is great with Arthur – although at first he could be a little bit heavy-handed. I would watch him and say: 'Paul, no.' Luckily, he does listen when he is told – I'm taking it as a good sign for the terrible twos! When we were on holiday in Dubai, all he wanted to do was kiss Arthur and play with his toes and give him his dummy. He loves Nelly too, and it's wonderful to see the cousins so close, it melts my heart. It makes me so excited to think about what is next for our family and what a wonderful big brother my baby Paul will be.

Bring on the future and more baby Knightleys!

Love, Sam x

August 2017

Crohn's and Pregnancy

I get asked about my experience of having Crohn's while being pregnant a lot, and so I felt it was important to have a section devoted to this topic. Because we hadn't spent ages looking into having a baby, I didn't have any anxiety about wondering if my condition would stop me from getting pregnant as it just happened! I did worry a bit about the disease affecting the actual pregnancy but I was reassured early on by medical professionals that, because I hadn't conceived in the middle of a flare-up, it shouldn't compromise the pregnancy at all, which it didn't. Many women get in touch with me through social media asking for advice on how I manage my condition, and I wanted to be 100 per cent clear on what is recommended for pregnant women who suffer from IBD, so I spoke to Crohn's and Colitis UK. When my pregnancy was announced, they released this statement:

Most women with Crohn's disease who are in remission or generally well when they conceive can expect to have a normal pregnancy and a healthy baby.

However, each woman's pregnancy will be individual to them and it is recommended that they speak to their healthcare professional as they may need to take special care with some aspects of their pregnancy.

We wish Sam all the best in her pregnancy.

If you have active IBD, especially Crohn's, there's a chance that you may have a slightly lower chance of conceiving. Severe inflammation in the small intestine can affect the fallopian tubes and make it more difficult to get pregnant. There is also some evidence linking Crohn's with a lower 'ovarian reserve'; in other words, eggs capable of being fertilised in women over 30.

The drugs prescribed for Crohn's – such as methotrexate, an immunosuppressant, and azathioprine (what I was on when I took medication for my condition) – can cause birth defects or miscarriages if taken when trying to conceive or while pregnant.

There have been a lot of studies looking at the effect of IBD on pregnancy, with different results. What does seem consistent is the link between IBD and early – or preterm – birth, babies with a low birth weight, and – sadly, but rarely – miscarriages.

However, several studies have shown that most women with IBD who are in remission or have only mild active disease at the time they conceive are very likely to have a normal uncomplicated pregnancy – like I was lucky enough to experience. And for women who remain in remission, the risk of problems such as miscarriage becomes the same for a woman without IBD. (Sadly, it's estimated that one in five of all pregnancies ends in miscarriage.)

You are also more likely to remain well if your symptoms are under control when you conceive.

This is why, if you are thinking of getting pregnant, most doctors will advise you to try to get your IBD under control first.

Research has also suggested that active disease at conception or flare-ups while pregnant may make you more likely to give birth early or have a low birth-weight baby. Severe active Crohn's disease or a very severe flare-up of ulcerative colitis (UC) may put you and the baby at greater risk. However, please be reassured that this does not always happen – many women who conceived when their disease was active or had a relapse while pregnant have gone on to have normal pregnancies and healthy babies. But, it is definitely better for you and your baby if you can keep in remission while you are pregnant. So, if your IBD symptoms begin to get worse, consult your doctor or IBD team as soon as possible.

Should I keep taking my medicine while I'm pregnant?

The studies I've read suggest that active Crohn's or UC may do more harm to the growing baby than most IBD medicines. So you'll probably be advised to continue taking your IBD medication during pregnancy. This is particularly important if you have had a recent flare-up and are trying to get it under control. This is definitely something you should consult with your doctor about.

A few drugs used for IBD are not recommended or should not be used at all by pregnant women. This means that if you are, or are planning to be, pregnant, it is important to check with your IBD team whether you need to change your drug treatment.

I was in the fortunate position of already having stopped taking my medication as I chose to manage my illness with diet, exercise and lots of natural remedies that Paul found for me when he was doing his research. As soon as we got together he made it his mission to educate us both about how I could keep Crohn's in remission without having to rely on drugs for the rest of my life. Touch wood, since the day I stopped my medication, I haven't had a big flare-up – in fact, I felt great and full of energy throughout my pregnancy. One tip that worked for me when it came to reacting quickly to early flare-up signs was, the minute I felt a single cramp or slightly unwell, I would cut out wheat completely for two weeks. Any pain or twinge went away immediately and it stopped whatever might be brewing right in its tracks.

What can I do to increase the chances of having a healthy baby?

Maintaining remission

If your disease is under control while you are pregnant then the baby is more likely to be healthy. So it's important to follow your treatment plan and to try and be as healthy as possible before and during your pregnancy.

Talk to your doctor if you have any worries about how to manage your IBD while pregnant. In particular, tell your doctor if you have a flare-up of your IBD or are failing to gain weight as expected.

Diet

For any pregnant woman, a balanced and varied diet with sufficient calories, vitamins and minerals is important for the growth of their baby. NHS Choices has a range of information on how to stay healthy while pregnant, including information on diets. If you're a pregnant women with IBD, the increased nutritional needs of pregnancy may mean you need to supplement your diet with extra vitamins and minerals, especially if you are underweight or have active disease. You may find it helpful to talk to a dietician or your IBD team about this.

You might be advised to take extra folic acid, which all women should take in their first 12 weeks of pregnancy. Folic acid – or vitamin B9 – helps reduce the risk of birth defects such as spina bifida. The usual recommended dose is 400 micrograms a day, but inflammation in the small intestine and some IBD drugs can affect how well you absorb folic acid. If you are on sulphasalazine, have Crohn's in the small intestine, or have had surgery to remove part of your small intestine, you may need a higher dose of folic acid, for example up to 5mg a day. Check with your doctor what dose of folic acid would suit you. You may also need extra vitamin B12, especially if you take extra folic acid.

I'm worried that pregnancy might make my ulcerative colitis or Crohn's disease worse

Try not to worry – most women with IBD go through their pregnancy without their IBD worsening. In fact, there has been research that suggests pregnancy might actually go some way to fixing the disease! For example, several studies have found that women with IBD had fewer relapses per year after having children than before they got pregnant.

How your IBD is likely to behave while you are pregnant appears to depend at least partly on how active your disease was when you started the pregnancy – luckily for me this wasn't an issue as I had been steadily well before I conceived baby Paul.

If you conceive when your IBD is in remission (inactive) you have a good chance of staying in remission. Studies have shown that about one in three women with UC who conceive while their disease is inactive will have a flare-up during their pregnancy.

Websites

As I have said a few times, the information in this book is just my own experience and not how everyone will do it. There are sections where I focus on my own attitude and approach to key issues, but I thought it would be helpful to give you a list of websites where you can double check advice directly from professionals too.

For more information on the topics mentioned in my book you can visit the following websites.

For any general healthcare questions I use the NHS website:
• www.nhs.uk

For more information on the National Childbirth Trust please visit:
• www.nct.org.uk

For more information on naturopath Dr. Wallach please visit:
• www.wallachonline.com

If you are concerned about your baby's wellbeing, you can use the following link for when best to call your doctor.
• www.babycentre.co.uk/a563663/when-to-call-the-doctor-for-parents-of-babies

For NHS recommended tips to keeping your child safe in the sun please visit:

- www.nhs.uk/Conditions/pregnancy-and-baby/Pages/safety-in-the-sun.aspx

If you would like to enroll in baby first aid courses please visit the St John Ambulance website:

- www.sja.org.uk

For more information on co-sleeping and the potential risks please visit the following:

- www.babycentre.co.uk/a558334/co-sleeping-and-safety

For more information on Crohn's disease, colitis or any other inflammatory bowel disease please visit the following website:

- www.crohnsandcolitis.org.uk

For more delicious recipes from Annabel Karmel please visit her website:

- www.annabelkarmel.com

For all other medical enquiries please contact your healthcare provider.

Acknowledgements

Obviously I have to start with my two Pauls:

Being a mummy is the best thing that's ever happened to me and I want to thank Paul for giving me the most perfect family and a wonderful baby. We might have started on the path to parenthood earlier than some, but you have been by my side through every minute and I love that we are learning together how to be the best parents we can. I look forward to lots more babies (we both want five!) and our lives together.

To baby Paul – thank you for being the most perfect baby I could imagine. You are beautiful, funny, sociable, so loving and our little Danger Mouse! We love you so much and we are so proud of you.

To my wonderful family:

Mum, you have been amazing from the minute we told you I was pregnant. Baby Paul and Nelly are so lucky to have you as a nanny and they love you.

Billie and Greg – thanks for doing it all first so that I knew what to expect! Nelly and her new little brother are so lucky to have you as parents and I will always treasure those early days with Nelly after she was born. They taught me so much and now I have had my own baby, I know how precious that early time is.

Gaynor – I can't thank you enough for all you do for me and my family. From day one you have welcomed me into your home and since we had the baby you are always there with advice and encouragement. Baby Paul is so lucky to have you in his life.

The rest of my family and friends have been amazing since I had baby Paul – thank you all so much for everything

Xanthe – we couldn't do it all without you! Thanks for being loyal and keeping everything going in our manic, crazy lives.

When it comes to books, I have worked with Carly Cook on them all and loved every second of each one. Thank you for being such a loyal friend and listening to me ramble on for hours about my life during our sessions. We are always on the same page and I love your drive and the faith you have in me.

My loyal fans are amazing and I know how lucky I am to have you all supporting and following me – thank you.

Thank you to everyone at Blink Publishing – it was such a big moment as writing about having a baby is so different from the other books I have done. But from the very first meeting (with lots of cake!) I just felt right at home. Huge thanks to my editor (and fellow new mum!) Kelly Ellis and to the rest of the team: Amy Llambias, Karen Browning, Lisa Hoare and everyone else who has helped bring the book together so quickly!

There have been some specific people who have helped with the more medical sections of this book:

Huge thanks to Crohn's and Colitis UK for their invaluable advice and guidelines on pregnancy and Crohn's – specific thanks to Sam Afhim and Andie Hill for their time and excellent advice.

Big thanks to Hannah Farrelly, registered midwife, for talking through some of the finer points of birth that I'd forgotten!

Thanks to Broomfield Hospital for the amazing care we received from all the doctors and the midwives who attended the actual birth. Even though I couldn't deliver at home, everyone at the hospital made it a positive and lovely experience and we are so grateful.

Huge thanks also to Sophie Bradshaw for helping me with some delicious recipes that we all love to eat as a family.

Lastly I just want to say this is what worked for me; it's not me telling you what to do or how to do it, it's just the book I wish I'd read when I was pregnant. All mummies know that we learn every day and all I know is that I love every second of being a mum to baby Paul. It's the best feeling in the world, and for that I am most grateful and thankful of all.

Picture Credits